THE BRITISH LIBRARY GUIDE TO

Bookbinding

THE BRITISH LIBRARY GUIDE TO

Bookbinding

HISTORY AND TECHNIQUES

P.J.M. Marks

UNIVERSITY OF TORONTO PRESS

FRONT COVER: Inset, *see* fig. 2.
Background from fig. 46.

HALF TITLE PAGE: *see* fig. 61.

FRONTISPIECE: Enlargement from fig. 36.

TITLE PAGE: Detail from fig. 53.

© 1998 The British Library Board

First published 1998 by
The British Library
96 Euston Road
London NW1 2DB

Published in North and South America in 1998 by
University of Toronto Press Incorporated
Toronto and Buffalo

Canadian Cataloguing in Publication Data

Marks, P. J. M. (Philippa J. M.)
    The Bitish Library Guide to Bookbinding:
    history and techniques

(The British Library Guides)
Includes bibliographical references.
ISBN 0-8020-8176-2

1. Bookbinding – History. 2. Bookbinding. I. Title.
II. Series

Z269M37 1998   686.3'009   C98-930806-5

Illustrations (figs 17, 18, 20, 21, 22, 26, 27, 29, 30
and 32) by Keith Banks.

Designed and typeset by Andrew Shoolbred
Colour origination by Culver Graphics
Printed in Italy by Grafiche Milani, Milan

Contents

Acknowledgements

I would like to express my gratitude to Dr Mirjam Foot for her guidance over the years and for her help with this book.

Thanks are also due to: Jean Archibald, Anne Barrett, Oliver Bettis, Patricia Bettis, Peter Carey, Mike Crump, Kevin Fromings, John Goldfinch, Kathleen Houghton, James Marks, Angela Newman, Deborah Novotny, Maurice Packer, Laurence Pordes, Gill Ridgley, Wan Lan Sng, David Way and Anne Young; also, to the staff of the British Library, the Bodleian Library, Maggs Brothers Ltd, and the National Art Library.

I am grateful to the following owners for permission to reproduce photographs of books in their collection:

British Library: figs 1–9, 13–16, 23, 24, 28, 31,32, 33–44, 47–51, 53–55, 57–64, 66–73, 75–80; Sotheby's: figs. 10, 74; Galleria Nazionale delle Marche, Urbino: fig. 11; Master and Fellows of Corpus Christi College, Cambridge: fig. 12; Conservatorio di Musica G B Martini, Bologna: fig. 25; Bodleian Library, Oxford: fig. 44; Trustees for Roman Catholic Purposes Registered: fig. 52; Pierpont Morgan Library, New York: fig. 56; Hispanic Society of America: fig. 65; Mrs Stanley Bray: fig. 45.

Introduction

Why are bookbindings of interest? Everyone can enjoy looking at a beautiful object, but in the case of a binding, the structure and craft of construction is concealed. I would like to explain how a book comes to be the way it is, within as well as without.

Is the task worth the effort? Until quite recently, even historians of the book trade tended to regard the subject of binding as a backwater, attracting the narrow specialist or the dilettante who revels in an arcane vocabulary of 'gauffering', 'hollow back' and 'Queens' Binder A'.

Yet the study of bindings may throw fascinating sidelights upon a wide range of cultural studies.[1] Aspects of art, literature, biography, sociology and economics can be illuminated from this seemingly unlikely angle. A binding may help date and place a manuscript, give information about trade routes and the spread of ideas, indicate its owner's social and economic status or aspirations, reflect contemporary artistic taste, indicate the significance of texts and the level of technology at a given time.

Until the nineteenth century, most books were not sold ready bound. Traditionally, books were transported as loose sheets in barrels or chests, some on a sale or return basis and only bound subsequently if required. Therefore a book published in Venice could be exported to England and bound there (sometimes many years after publication) in a style to suit the taste and purse of the purchaser. There was a steady demand for classical texts, prayerbooks, almanacs and school books, so booksellers would have had stocks of these to sell ready-bound. Binding history reflects the trends of European history; witness the spread of Empire-style bindings into the northern Italian states in the wake of Napoleon, and the impact of the English industrial revolution on the hand-binding trade.

1. Early methods of book storage. Jan Amos Komensky, *Orbis sensualium pictus*, London, 1672, p.196. BL 1607/2351.

No one would dispute the importance of books in the development of western culture. It is the binding which has given us the conventional image of a book. Elements such as the raised bands on the spine of a binding are functional, not purely decorative. An article in *The Bookbinder* of 1888 notes that 'a gilt edge is as necessary to a well-bound book as the gold chain is to an alderman's robes.'[2] But it also has the practical function of protecting the contents from dust.

The way a book was bound can also tell us how it was used. Many pre-sixteenth-century bindings were not shelved upright, but stored flat either on a lectern or a shelf with the edges of the text facing outwards (*see* fig. 1). This is indicated by the undecorated spines, the elaborate bosses and metalwork on the covers (to protect them while lying flat) and by the fact that the title was often written in ink horizontally on the fore-edge of the text. The type of readership can also dictate the format of a book. With the advent of printing and the increased demand for scholarly texts inspired by the Italian Renaissance, books became smaller and lighter. They were no longer chained up for consultation in institutional libraries but could be carried in the owner's pocket.

The binders as individuals are not without interest – for example, Jean de Planche, binder and bigamist; Roger Payne, whose 'reputation has been enhanced by his partiality for strong drink and his elaborate, not always truthful, bills'[3]; Christophe Plantin, whose binding career ended in a brawl with a drunken nobleman; and Thomas Elliott, who revenged himself on a complaining client by incorporating the letters of his own name into the design of two bindings![4]

A sixteenth-century binder would be familiar with many of the tools and techniques used today. However, then as now, binders have their own ways of doing things, and one must allow for individual preferences; for example, the way the covers were attached might differ from workshop to workshop in the same town.

This study does not aim to be comprehensive but to provide clues for the amateur. It is not an instruction manual. Many practical guides have been written, dating from the tenth century onwards.[5] The emphasis is on the history of western bindings with a bias towards

England; oriental binding has its own traditions. The earliest practices cannot be described with certainty, as relatively few pre-tenth-century bindings survive and these examples may not be representative. Many later practices associated with nineteenth-century machine binding rather than hand binding are only briefly touched upon. A detailed treatment of the whole field has not been possible due to limitations of space. It is hoped that the Further Reading section (p. 92) may go some way towards providing further guidance.

2. A sixteenth-century German workshop with binders 'forwarding'. Hans Sachs, *Eygentliche Beschreibung aller Stände auff Erden*, Frankfurt, 1568, p.11. BL C.57.b.25.

Bookbinding today does not enjoy a glamorous image. It is no surprise to find characters in an Alan Bennett play attending evening classes in the subject, but learning that Picasso and Matisse created designs for bindings gives a different perspective. Royalty, aristocrats, civil servants, scholars, and churchmen have all been associated with fine bindings. These include King Matthias Corvinus of Hungary, Francis I and Henry II of France, Diane of Poitiers, the Medici family, John Evelyn, Cardinal Richelieu, Queen Christina of Sweden, Pope Clement IX, Napoleon, George III, Catherine the Great of Russia, and William Morris. Many would recognise the sentiment which inspired an expedition of Samuel Pepys, described in his diary: 'After that to a booksellers and bought, for the love of the binding, three books.'[6]

Bookbinding terms: forwarding and finishing

Bookbinding is the process whereby the pages of a manuscript or printed book are secured in a particular order and encased by protective covers.

Charles Lamb wrote: 'To be strong-backed and neat-bound is the desideratum of a volume. Magnificence comes after.'[7] The technical process of binding a book reflects this. It is split into two stages: 'forwarding', the sewing of the leaves and attachment of the covers (*see* fig. 2); and 'finishing', the decoration of the covers, commonly achieved by the impression of brass tools (*see* fig. 3). Other technical terms are explained in the Glossary (p. 88).

3. A modern binder decorating the spine, i.e. 'finishing'.

Historical outline

The codex evolved during the first century AD and was the predecessor of modern book structures; before then, scrolls and writing tablets were in use. The codex comprised two boards enclosing sheets and the whole structure was sewn at the back. The codex developed over the years, the sewing attaching the sheets became more sophisticated, and decorated leather or cloth covered the boards. As has been mentioned, relatively few pre-tenth-century bindings survive, so it is difficult to determine whether the techniques used in their construction are representative of the craft at that particular time.

The sheets of the codex were initially made of papyrus, which was gradually replaced in the fourth century by parchment, a translucent material made from prepared animal skins. Paper, made in China c.104 AD, was not manufactured in Europe until the twelfth century. Paper began to replace parchment with the introduction of printing in the middle of the fifteenth century, since by then paper was quicker and cheaper to make. It was also easier to print on to paper than on vellum.

The interest in studying classical texts that underlay the Italian Renaissance caused an increased demand for books, which became more plentiful and cheaper to produce after the advent of printing. Political and religious proseletysers used the printed word to further their own causes – for example the pamphlets and books produced by the Protestant religious reformers of the sixteenth century and the advocates of the Counter Reformation. Such activity stimulated all areas of the book trade.

Increased demand resulted in the development of techniques, involving both the structure and decoration of the binding, to speed up the work. Short-cuts were found in the sewing processes and rolls and panel stamps were increasingly used in place of time-consuming tooling with small, individual stamps. Fundamental change, however, did not come about until the industrial revolution of the nineteenth century. Machines were invented which allowed the text blocks and cases to be produced separately and in quantity. The binding trade diverged into craft workshops, which produced a relatively small number of unique bindings made by hand in the traditional way; and large mechanised workshops capable of producing whole editions of a publisher's work in leather, cloth or paper and at a low cost.

Uses and design

The structure and decoration of a binding depends on its use. A pre-fifteenth century religious text to be used by the clergy would have heavy wooden boards with clasps to keep the vellum pages flat and bosses to protect the covers from the lectern or shelf on which it was stored. A school text book would be bound in cheap leather with minimal decoration. An illuminated manuscript, bound as a gift from one monarch to another, would require the most costly materials and lavish decoration.

A design can be influenced by many factors: the artistic trends of a particular nation or period, the skill and vision of the binder, the demands of the patron, the quality of the materials used, and even the political climate (the trade in leather, for example, was sometimes disrupted by war).

HISTORY
The bookbinding trade

The bookbinding trade in Europe

The trade of bookbinding was influenced by many factors differing according to period and local circumstance, and it is impossible to offer a comprehensive study which would be universally applicable. Broad areas have been chosen for discussion, although some specific examples of the type of incident important in a binder's life, whenever and wherever he lived, are also given.

Christopher de Hamel in his *Scribes and Illuminators* (1992) notes that Saint Osmund, eleventh-century bishop of Salisbury, is recorded as having bound books for the cathedral with his own hands. This reflects the close connection between the Church and the craft of binding. Curiously, the Church both provided and supplied the market. Many early bindings were made by monks for monasteries and other religious foundations. Reading, writing and study were considered sacred duties, as were the associated tasks of illumination and binding. Texts were also required for teaching purposes, since most educational institutions were run by the Church, which supplied the royal courts with administrators as well as priests. Developments such as the emergence of cathedral schools in Paris in the twelfth century, the monastic revival which spread across Europe in the same century, and the Reformation of the sixteenth century, stimulated all aspects of the book trade.

Binding was not to be exclusively a monastic business. In Paris, during the late twelfth and early thirteenth centuries, stationers commissioned different craftsmen to copy and to bind texts, thus separating these activities. Secular binderies developed to meet the needs of other people who used books, such as lawyers, students, civil servants and businessmen. As was the case for most craft activities, the trade was usually regulated by guilds or other organisations, for example the Guild of St Luke in the Netherlands, the Stationers' Company in England, the Confrèrie des Libraires, Relieurs, Enlumineurs, Ecrivains et Parcheminiers (the Confraternity of Booksellers, Bookbinders, lluminators, Scribes and Parchment makers) in France and local organisations ('Innung') in the German states.

The organisation of work differed according to period and local custom. Until the nineteenth century, an English binder would carry out all stages of the binding process himself. Later, craftsmen in larger workshops were frequently allotted different tasks ('finishers' being paid more than 'forwarders'). In Germany, a single worker was responsible for all the processes involved. In France, a differentiation was usually made between 'relieurs', who made the structure of the binding and 'doreurs', who gold-tooled the covers (and individual workmen could hire out their services to several workshops).

The fact that businessmen supplied bindings does not necessarily mean that they were binders themselves. The printer Thomas Berthelet is recorded as having provided Henry VIII with bindings. The assumption has been made that Berthelet was also a binder but there is no proof to suggest he did more than arrange for the books to be bound. Successful binders tended to become businessmen and, although they owned their own workshops, would not have worked at the bench themselves.

Binding shops grew up near their markets. Towns and cities with royal residences, or important government, legal, religious and edu-cational institutions would also be centres of binding. Binderies were located near the booksellers and stationers who provided most of their custom. In London, the area around St Paul's Cathedral was devoted to the book trade. Busy thoroughfares like Paternoster Row were lined with booksellers', stationers' and printers' premises, with the side alleys like Ivy Lane and Ave Maria Lane housing the binderies (since binders did not rely on passing trade). In Paris, binderies clustered around such streets as Sept-Voies, St Jacques, and St Jean-de-Beauvais. In an attempt to protect local workers, foreign binders were often required by law to work in specified locations away from the major areas of trade (in sixteenth-century London, these were called 'liberties' and included St Martin's le Grand, Blackfriars, Southwark and West-minster) and were denied the privileges enjoyed by indigenous

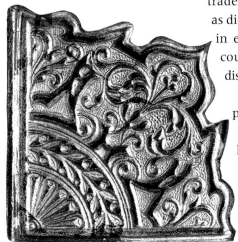

4. Cornerpiece gold-tooled on the binding of Erasmus, *Adagiorum Chiliades,* [Frankfurt] 1559 by Williamson of Eton. BL C.128.k.3.

tradesmen. However, foreign workers could also thrive, as did the German immigrant binders who led the trade in eighteenth-century London. The term 'foreigner' could also apply to tradesmen from another town or district within the same country.

There was always a market for binders in the provinces. Work was usually less sophisticated and styles, copied from the leading city binders, were a little old-fashioned. On leaving school at Eton in 1604, Charles Somerset had his books bound by a local binder, probably Vincent Williamson (often mentioned in binding literature), described as 'a good workeman but he hath commonly his hands full of worke, and his head full of drinck. Yet I had as leve venture my worke with this good fellow that is sometime sober, as with them that are always mad'[8] (*see* fig. 4). Many provincial binders were capable of original and accomplished work; the Worcester binder, John Holl, for example, who worked for Queen Victoria.

A binder's life

Binderies were frequently small establishments until the nineteenth century, when many processes came to be mechanised, enabling the mass production of bindings. Before then, the qualified binder (called a 'Freeman' in England) often lived above his workshop with his family and an apprentice or two. During the day, he was helped by a journeyman (a qualified binder who could not yet afford his own business). Hours were long; in the early eighteenth century, a London binder could expect to work from six in the morning to nine at night, six days a week; a hundred years later, the working day ended at six. A journeyman might have to travel the country in search of work. It was not uncommon for German journeymen to work abroad for a year. This period was known as the 'wanderjahre'.

Even established binders had to travel to where the work was and this explains the immigration of German binders into eighteenth-century London, where English bibliophiles could afford to pay for de luxe bindings. One such, Andreas Linde, produced work for the Prince of Wales, later George III. Unlike some professions, the tools of a binder's trade could be carried around relatively easily. Some binders were required to travel to the houses of wealthy book collectors and to

14

carry out the work of binding or restoring the books on the premises.

'As to the Work itself, though a great many Parts of it are seemingly but piddling, yet there are others that are laborious, and together they require a Lad of Strength, as well as to be ready and neat in his working.'[9] This lad was the unwaged apprentice who received instruction in binding and 'meat, drink, apparell, lodging and all other necessaries' often in return for a premium paid by his parents (although sometimes this was waived)[10]. The treatment of the apprentice depended on the good nature of the binder and his family. A Victorian binder, John Jaffray, noted 'Mother Remnant used to feed the apprentices very queerly. It was a common observation of hers that there was 'no butter in the house – there will be some more in tomorrow.'[11] At the age of 21 or over and after his training (commonly seven years), the English apprentice could apply to the guild for permission to practise binding in his own right. Eventually, he might be able to set up his own shop and take on apprentices himself. In this way, the skills of the trade were passed down the generations. A direct line of apprenticeship can be traced from Robert Steele, who began work in the establishment of Charles II's binder, Samuel Mearne, in the seventeenth century, to John Lovejoy (known for Masonic bindings) in the nineteenth century (*see* fig. 5). From the late nineteenth century, it became possible to learn binding at art schools and, as the system of apprenticeship declined, more binders trained at these institutions.

An easy way for an apprentice or journeyman to further his career was to marry the daughter or widow of a binder who owned his own shop. This was probably the case with royal binder Augustin Duseuil who married Françoise, the daughter of the binder Philip Padeloup, in 1699. Binderies were frequently family businesses. Trade in France from the seventeenth to eighteenth centuries was dominated by the family firms of the aforementioned Padeloup, and also those of Derome and LeMonnier.

It cost less for a boy to learn binding than related trades because prospects for financial advancement were not so favourable. At a time in England when meat could be purchased for a few pennies a pound and a week's lodgings

5. Masonic motif gold-tooled on the binding of *The Holy Bible*, Oxford, 1808 by Lovejoy.
BL C.155.a.8.

6. Full black Turkey (goatskin) binding, tooled in gold and onlaid, on *Book of Common Prayer*, London, 1662 by Samuel Mearne. Although Charles II's cypher is featured, his coat of arms has been replaced by that of a later monarch, the bibliophile George III. BL C.14.e.13.

could be had for three shillings, a journeyman earned about twelve shillings a week. A mason (who would have had comparable skills) received fifteen to eighteen shillings.

Qualified binders often took on extra work as stationers and/or booksellers to supplement their income and to increase their social standing. The binder Claude Picques was also bookseller to Queen Cathérine de Medici. Samuel Mearne held the offices of Bookbinder, Bookseller and Stationer to King Charles II, and also had a share in a printing house (*see* fig. 6). The London printer and stationer John Dunton (1659–1733) wrote of his chief binder, Thomas Axe, 'notwithstanding his losses in trade, I believe Mr Axe will get money enough; for he is not only a good Binder, but sells Books, Globes, Auctions.'[12] Ludovicus Ravescot, binding in Louvain at the end of the fifteenth century, was also an illuminator and printer. Baldassarre Scariglia (who ran the court bindery until 1492) and Lucas Weischner (died 1609) combined their binding activities with librarianship, working for the Aragonese King of Naples and the University of Jena respectively.

It was useful to have other skills to fall back on when trade was bad; for example, there was little call for elaborate bindings during the French Revolution. A simple example is shown (*see* fig. 7). Some ways of supplementing income had nothing to do with the book trade. William Codd, a binder in Bridgetown, Barbados, announced on his trade ticket 'Panama hats neatly dressed'.[13] When times were hard in nineteenth-century Paris, Lesné relied on his carpentry skills. Others gave up binding altogether. John Dunton wrote of his binder, Mr Mahood, 'From Book-binding he went to the Garter Coffee-house by the Royal Exchange; and I hope he has thrived at it.'[14]

It was important to judge the market correctly and supply what people wanted. Sometimes the taste was for novelty (for example the translucent vellum bindings of Edwards of Halifax (*see* fig. 51) and nineteenth-century bindings made of papier mâché), sometimes it was backward-looking (for example, the retrospective bindings made by Joseph Thouvenin (*see* fig. 74) for the French academician and author, Charles Nodier). On occasion, binders only had to please themselves or their families. It is likely that the Amsterdam binder, Albert Magnus, bound the beautifully gold-tooled Bible he gave to his wife as a wedding present in 1670.

There was always a reason why a binder bound a book in a particular way. The binder's aim would be to complete the work as quickly as possible using appropriate materials for the job. He might take short cuts to save time and money. This can be seen when printing became widespread and the demand for books increased. Binders would sometimes sew several sections of text on at once, tie

7. Central motif gold-
tooled on the binding of
*Étrennes intéressantes des
quatre parties du Monde,*
Paris, 1792.
BL Davis 571.

headbands down less frequently or even use stuck-
on headbands.

Although the best advertisement of a binder's
skill were the bindings themselves, Roger Payne
(1739–1797) did not trust the patron to sufficiently
appreciate his genius (*see* fig. 8). Many of his elaborate and rather self-congratulatory bills still exist,
together with the bindings. He wrote of the copy of
Lilly's *Christian Apology* (now owned by the Grolier
Club of New York) 'Bound in the very best
manner... it is absolutely a very Extra Bound Book. I
hope to be forgiven for saying so and unmatch-
able.'[15] Payne was not above admitting his mistakes,
however, and his errors often reflected absentmind-
edness rather than lack of skill (although some have
accused him of insobriety!). Forgetting to refer to
the original order, Payne used the incorrect tools
and 'Finished Fuller [T. Fuller, *The History of the Worthies of England*
(London, 1662)] according to y^e . Taste for English History with oak
Leaves [and] Acorns;' and was forced to 'sett a smaller price on y^e.
Bookbinding than I can well afford to do. The Book being Bound so
remarkable Well.'[16]

Gaining an official appointment to a king, queen, prince or aristo-
cratic family was a great advantage, even if payment was sometimes
dilatory (on several occasions Charles II's binder, Samuel Mearne,
refused to return books until his bill was settled).[17] The king's binder
would not only supply the royal library, he would also bind official
documents and books to be presented as gifts. The regulations of religious or chivalric orders founded by royalty also required impressive
bindings. French royal binders Nicholas Eve (died 1581) and Clovis
Eve (probably father and son), bound several copies of the statutes
relating to the Order of the Holy Spirit, founded by Henry III in 1578.[18]
It was Henry, too, who established associations to promote the
Counter Reformation in France. Religious works were bound for
these associations in an appropriately sober style, featuring skulls,
coffins and skeletons. The silver-tooled motif illustrated here (*see* fig.
9) comes from the binding of *L'office de la Vierge Marie*, Paris, 1586
bound for a member of the Compagnie des Confrères de la Mort.

A royal warrant could also provide an element of protection.

Binders in sixteenth-century Dresden resented the success of the court binders Jacob Krause and Caspar Meuser and refused to acknowledge Meuser as a Master Binder. These two were considered 'foreign' as they were not Dresden-born. The Elector of Saxony, August I, supported his binders and threatened to abolish the binders' guild stating that Meuser's 'work is better than any of you and he has been working for such a long time with our bookbinder [Krause], behaving in an honest and pious way... So shall the work commend its master, whose craft is most skilled.'[19] When Meuser died, the Elector refused to appoint a replacement, and instead provided work for Meuser's widow who ran the workshop with the help of a journeyman.

It is difficult to establish the exact position of the binder in society, and there were national differences. Samuel Pepys's direct interest in bookbinding has already been noted but it is clear that the more successful he became in his career, the less he associated with the binders themselves. The writings of the Victorian binder, John Jaffray, also shed light on the situation. Although the social standing of stationers, booksellers and printers was higher, some binders did enjoy a certain status. Jaffray noted that German binders 'fancy themselves and are allowed by others to be a better sort of people than the common run of mechanics... If a cobbler or tailor goes into a wine room they are looked upon as nothing ... but a binder meets with civility from everyone.'[20] (Jaffray also provides an interesting statistic. In 1840, 218 bookbinders were taken into custody by the Metropolitan Police, compared with 2043 tailors and 88 goldbeaters, the highest and lowest number of offenders listed by profession).[21]

If binders were not very high up the social scale, some had aspirations. Charles Lewis (1786–1836) was light-heartedly criticised for wearing tassels to his high boots, presumably the prerogative of a gentleman.[22] Social niceties meant little to Roger Payne, who, 'proud of his talents and regardless of his dress', thought nothing of bursting into Countess Spencer's dressing room.[23] This did not prejudice his

8. Constantine Lascaris, *Erotemata*, Venice, 1494 bound by Roger Payne. The arms of the Rev. C.M. Cracherode are on the upper cover. The small tools, high headbands and dark end-leaves (frequently purple) are characteristic of Payne's work at this time. BL IA 24382.

9. Skeleton motif, silver-tooled on the binding of *L'office de la Vierge Marie*, Paris, 1586. BL C.129.mm.4.

10. O. Uzanne, *The Sunshade*, London, 1883 bound by Rivière & Son with watercolours painted on ivory by Mrs C B Currie. Photograph courtesy of Sotheby's, London.

case, as the second Earl Spencer (1758–1834, perhaps the foremost collector of the day) was an enthusiastic patron.

Even if the binders themselves were not personally in demand in the highest circles, their skill was. Sumptuous bindings enhanced the image of royal courts, so rulers sometimes went to great lengths to secure the services of the most capable practitioners. In the 1780s, Catherine the Great tried to lure Christian Samuel Kalthoeber 'who is undoubtedly now the finest bookbinder in the world' according to contemporary writer J.C. Hüttner,[24] to move from London to St Petersburg, but without success.

Less fortunate sections of society were sometimes taught binding as a means of earning a living. In nineteenth-century England, women off the streets learned the trade in a Hackney workshop, sponsored by the Salvation Army; orphans and poor apprentices were similarly instructed in Paris. (A copy of Chomel's *Des fièvres de des maladies pestilentielles* (Paris, 1821), has the trade ticket of the Manufacture Général des Apprentis Pauvres et Orphelins). The binder Lesné taught binding at the Deaf and Dumb Institute in Paris. There are records of binders with disabilities, such as a French deaf and dumb binder called Maynard (perhaps taught by Lesné), and Nathaniel Price, a blind journeyman who worked in London for Edward Curtis and Son and signed his bindings 'N.PRICE (Perfectly dark)'.[25]

Women bookbinders

There are early references to woman binders, notably a 'Dionisia le Bokebyndere' in fourteenth-century London and Marguerite, who appears in the accounts of the Duke of Normandy in 1459. Jane Steel, daughter of Robert Steel (once apprenticed to Samuel Mearne), ran one of the most successful binding shops in early eighteenth-century London and bills survive with details of her work. Widows were also well placed to take over binders' workshops. When Nicolas-Denis Derome died in about 1788, his Paris business was taken over by his widow and her son-in-law, Bradel, who signed their bindings with a ticket printed 'Veuve Derome et Bradel son gendre'. The women did

THE SUNSHADE

MUFF AND GLOVE

not necessarily work at the bench themselves, although some undoubtedly did. Mrs Weir, married to the binder Weir (known as Davy or Richard Weir, sometimes spelt Wier, died 1792), who worked with Roger Payne, bound books but was perhaps better known as a paper restorer. According to John Jaffray 'She went down to repair, wash and mend the MSS. of the Society of Writers to the Signet in Edinburgh at a salary of £1.1.0 per week, where she died'.[26]

Historically, women were employed in binderies for sewing and headbanding. These were women who needed to work for their living. In the nineteenth century, middle-class women became binders in their own right, some learning from teachers as distinguished as Thomas James Cobden-Sanderson, a friend of William Morris. In a fourteen-year period at his Doves Bindery, Cobden-Sanderson (see fig. 77) taught more than twelve women students, mostly Americans. Courses were also run by institutions, both in London (for example, the Guild of Women Binders), and in the provinces by the Home Arts and Industries Association.[27] From the turn of the century, increasing numbers of women learnt the craft at art schools including the Ecole et Les Ateliers d'Art Décoratif in Paris.

Women were sometimes associated with the painting of bindings and fore-edges. Dr Johnson's friend, Mrs Thrale, mentions having seen a lady painting the covers of a vellum binding and refers to 'a beautiful Miniature Landscape painted likewise by the Lady.'[28] (Painted vellum bindings and fore-edges like these are associated with the Edwards of Halifax bindery.) Women still carried out such tasks at the beginning of the twentieth century. Miss C.B. Currie produced many signed fore-edges and was also responsible for miniature portraits on 'Cosway' bindings sold by the London bookshop, Sotheran's (see fig. 10).

Patrons of bookbinding
According to Gabriel Naudé, writing in the seventeenth century, 'it becomes the ignorant only to esteem a book for its cover'.[29] Nevertheless, many collectors did prize their bindings highly. They loved the art of binding for its own sake and wanted their collections to include examples by the most accomplished binders. Pepys was keen to have a book bound by Nott (probably William Nott) 'the famous bookbinder, that bound for my lord Chancellor's library; and here did I take occasion for curiosity to bespeak a book to be bound, only that I might have one of his binding'.[30]

Collecting historic bindings is a relatively recent occupation. In the past, many owners wanted their books to be bound or rebound in the latest style by the foremost binders. A well-known collector and secretary to Cathérine de Medici, Thomas Mahieu, did not preserve the original binding of his copy of *Hypnerotomachia Poliphili* (Venice, 1499) but had it rebound in the latest style by Claude Picques (*c.*1510–75), one of the best binders of the day (*see* fig. 64 for a Picques binding for Mahieu).[31] Today, collectors usually want to own examples of the work of notable binders, both historic and modern, and preserve bindings in their original condition, rather than have books rebound.

A contemporary description of the library of Federigo da Montefeltro (1422–82) is significant because it shows how bindings conveyed an image. When Federigo was created first Duke of Urbino, his family was considered 'new money' by the older dynasties.

11. Pedro Berruguete (died *c.*1504), *Federigo da Montefeltro and his son Guidobaldo*. Montefeltro is surrounded by his prize possessions, including a bound book.

Photograph courtesy of the Galleria Nazionale delle Marche, Urbino.

One way to establish status was to found a great library. Federigo's book buyer wrote: 'The Duke having completed his library at the great cost of thirty thousand ducats determined to give every writer a worthy finish by binding his work in scarlet and silver. Beginning with the Bible, as the cornerstone of this collection, he had it covered with gold brocade, and then he bound in scarlet and silver the Greek and Latin doctors and philosophers, the histories, the books on medicine and the modern doctors, a rich and magnificent sight.'[32] A beautifully bound book was a work of art, indicating the owner's taste, wealth and social position. In portraits, aristocrats like Federigo were often shown holding finely bound books (*see* fig. 11). The brocade-bound Bible demonstrated Federigo's piety, the classical texts his erudition. We know which books were considered important by the fact that they were given expensive coverings.

Some bibliophiles who travelled had books bound in whichever country they found themselves at the time. Cousins Damianus Pflug and Nicolas von Ebeleben were German students who travelled throughout Europe in the 1540s and commissioned bindings in the various places they visited. Fortunately

12. Caius, *De antiquitate Cantabrigiensis Academiae*, London, 1574 bound by Matthew Parker's Private Bindery to a corner and centrepiece design with a semis of diamond-shaped motifs.

Photograph courtesy of the Parker Library, Corpus Christi College, Cambridge.

for binding historians, their names, the name of the town, and date, were tooled onto the covers. Their collections included examples from Paris and Bologna. Furthermore, Pflug owned a Roman binding by Maestro Luigi (who bound for the Vatican and also produced 'Apollo and Pegasus' plaquette bindings (*see* fig. 60) for one of the most-talked about collections in binding history, owned by the banker G.B. Grimaldi). The Parisian bindings of Peter Ernst, Count von Mansfeld (1517–1604), general to the Holy Roman Emperor Charles V, date from the time he was imprisoned in the fortress of Vincennes after losing a battle to the French. His books, bound in the leading Paris workshops, no doubt provided great comfort (as did the presence of his cook, a fool, a greyhound and a parrot!). It is not known whether Mansfeld selected the books or whether they were a gift.[33] Those who could not travel used agents to obtain bindings from abroad, for example the Holy Roman Emperor's Chancellor, Cardinal Granvelle (1517–86) who, while Bishop of Arras, commissioned bindings from Venice.[34]

The English seventeenth-century diarist John Evelyn recommended that libraries should contain binding equipment including 'Skrew-presses, All of the Tooles belonging to the Binding of Books, Cyfers, Coats of Armes, Stamp letters, figures, Gilding tooles, Glew-pots, Cizers, knives &c'.[35] Other patrons went further.

The enthusiasm of Matthew Parker, Archbishop of Canterbury, for binding is indicated both by his patronage of the finest London workshops and by the establishment of his own bindery at Lambeth Palace. He wrote to Lord Burghley in 1572 'I have within my house in wagis, drawers & cutters, paynters, lymners, wryters, and boke bynders'[36] (*see* fig.12).

A personal bindery (at work from the 1780s–1820s) was also set up by George III. Many of the finishing tools used are now at Windsor Castle. The King had a disconcerting habit of dropping in on his binders during their break, on one occasion disturbing them frying sprats for their lunch.[37] Such was George's zeal that his bindery attracted the notice of a contemporary poet, Peter Pindar (the pseudonym of physician and poet, John Wolcot), who wrote:

> And yet our Monarch has a world of books
> And daily on their backs so gorgeous looks;
> So neatly bound, so richly gilt, so fine,
> He fears to open them to read a line!.....
> But here's the dev'l – I fear many know it–
> *Some* Kings prefer the *Binder* to the *Poet.*[38]

There is 'no furniture so charming as books' wrote the essayist Sydney Smith,[39] and bindings were often used as interior decoration. The style of bindings in the library of the Constable of France, Anne de Montmorency (1493–1567), matched the decor of his house at Ecouen. Pepys mentions a 'bill for the rebinding of some old books, to make them suit with my study, cost me (besides other new books in the same bill) 3*l* – but it will be very handsome.'[40]

People who commissioned bindings were not always wealthy. In seventeenth-century England, Elkanah Settle (1648–1724), a hack poet and dramatist, tried to make money by composing verse dedicated to members of the nobility (*see* fig. 13). The poems were specially bound with the appropriate coat-of-arms tooled on the cover. If the potential patron rejected the work, Settle merely replaced the dedication and coat-of-arms with those of another, hopefully more generous, aristocrat. On one binding there is evidence that the dedication and coat-of-arms had been changed three times!

Authors sometimes used fine bindings to promote their writing. Lord Herbert of Cherbury (1582/3–1648), needing patronage, had twenty copies of his treatise *De Veritate* specially bound for presentation to scholars and influential people (probably including Charles I). The binder he patronised also produced other work for the king and was named the Squirrel Binder after two characteristic tools.

Splendid bindings were often commissioned by individuals to be given as gifts to ensure good will or patronage. The library of Elizabeth I's favourite courtier, Robert Dudley, Earl of Leicester, contained fine bindings made by the best London workshops

13. Cherub's head motif gold-tooled on the binding of [Elkanah Settle], *A Pindaric Poem*, London, 1711.
BL C.66.f.24.

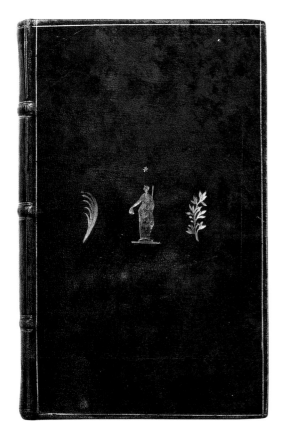

14. Emblematic motifs gold-tooled on the binding of John Toland, *Life of John Milton*, London, 1761 bound for Thomas Hollis. BL Davis 163.

of the day. Many were presentation copies – an indication of Dudley's perceived importance. Institutions also commissioned fine bindings. On the occasion of Charles II's restoration to the English throne in 1660, the Stationers' Company presented him with a copy of Foxe's *Book of Martyrs* specially bound by John Fletcher. On the fore-edge of the book there is a portrait of Charles and the signature 'FLETCHER COMPINXIT'.

The level of interest on the part of the patron varied considerably. Some noble collectors contented themselves with having the spines of their ancestral libraries re-tooled, since only the backs were visible. Bibliophiles like Jean Grolier (1479–1565) and Edward, Lord Harley (1689–1741), made their views known as to style and decoration. The English antiquarian, Sir Robert Bruce Cotton (1571– 1631), wrote instructions to the binder on the end-leaves of his books. He was concerned with both structure; 'Bind this book as strong as you can ... let it be shewed [sewed] withe 3 double threds waxed' and decoration; 'sett flowers of gold one the back and corners and mak it very fayre'.[41]

Decorative requirements were sometimes quite specific. Thomas Hollis, the eighteenth-century dissenter, distributed books to libraries abroad, notably the Harvard College Library. Hollis considered the decoration of the binding to be so important that he commissioned G.B. Cipriani to make designs for a set of binding tools which would enhance the libertarian theme of the books. The emblematic motifs featured, amongst others, Britannia, Liberty the owl, the caduceus, and the palm leaf (*see* fig.14). When the tools were damaged by fire, Hollis even had a second set cut.

Many interesting amateurs have been associated with the craft of bookbinding. In 1626, Nicholas Ferrar established a lay religious community in Little Gidding, Huntingdonshire. Male and female alike were engaged in the compilation and binding of Bibles and prayer books (*see* fig. 15), reviving the early monastic notion that such an occupation was a sacred duty. They were instructed in a variety of techniques by a binder's daughter from Cambridge, the home of several accomplished binders. A comment by the historian Thomas Fuller – 'their own Needles were emploied in learned and pious work to binde Bibles: Whereof one most exactly done was presented to King Charles'[42] probably refers to the sewing of the text, but has led to the erroneous belief, perpetuated in many booksellers' catalogues, that the community produced embroidered bindings.

Eminent individuals in many walks of life have been interested in the craft of bookbinding. In the twentieth century practitioners have

15. *The Actions & Doctrine & other Passages touching our Lord & Saviour*, [Little Gidding, 1635] bound by the Little Gidding community for Charles I. BL C.23.e.4.

included Queen Victoria's granddaughter, Princess Victoria of Wales, Virginia Woolf, and Vanessa Bell. Sir Edward Sullivan (died 1928) was a noted Irish barrister who was interested in both the craft and history of binding (*see* fig.16). He practised tooling in gold, signing his work E.S.AURIFEX'(E.S being his initials and 'aurifex' indicating that he was responsible for the gold-tooling). According to Sullivan, binding as a craft had become sterile and he, like Cobden-Sanderson, wanted to promote originality of design, declaring 'I see no reason why Ireland should not take the lead in changing all of this'.[43]

16. Floral motifs gold-tooled on the binding of Walter Crane, *A Masque of flowers*, London, 1889 by Sir Edward Sullivan.
BL Davis 269.

TECHNIQUES
Forwarding

Hand-binding techniques have changed little since the sixteenth century, so although some of the following descriptions are in the present tense, the information relates to past practices as well.*

Papyrus, parchment and paper

The sheets of the codex, which evolved in the first century AD, could be made of either papyrus (taken from the papyrus plant abundant around the Nile basin) or parchment (a translucent material made from prepared animal skins). Parchment refers to split skin obtained from a sheep or goat, whereas vellum comes from unsplit calfskin. (Sometimes the term 'vellum' is used to describe calfskin and 'parchment' is used when referring to the skin of other animals). By the fourth century, hard-wearing parchment was common.

The craft of papermaking (known in China since the first century), was not practised in Europe until the twelfth century. Handmade paper was made from pulped rags by dipping a wire mesh tray (called a mould) into a vat containing the fibrous pulp and water. The mould was removed and shaken so that the fibres drained and lay flat. The wet sheet was pressed and dried. A mixture called size was added to give a non-absorbent surface.

Handmade, or 'laid', paper contains two sets of lines visible when the sheet is held up to the light. The widely-spaced lines are called chain lines and the fainter, closely-set lines are wire (or laid) lines. These are made by the imprint of the mould.

*There are few authoritative accounts of the history of binding technique and the information in the following section owes a great deal to Bernard Middleton's *A History of English Craft Bookbinding Technique,* 4th rev. ed., (1996).

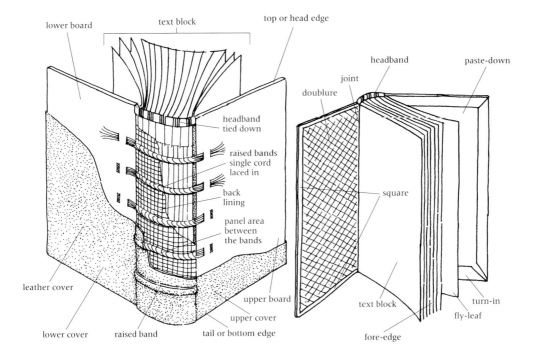

lower board

text block

top or head edge

headband

paste-down

joint

doublure

headband
tied down

raised bands
single cord
laced in

back
lining

panel area
between
the bands

square

leather cover

upper board

upper cover

turn-in

text block

fly-leaf

lower cover

raised band

tail or bottom edge

fore-edge

17. The structure of a
binding.

Wove paper, invented in the middle of the eighteenth century, does not feature these lines (unless they have been added artificially) since the mould was made of closely woven wires.

The rough, feathery edges of handmade paper are described as 'deckle'. The deckle is a frame which confines the paper pulp to the mould. Deckle edges can also be introduced artificially in machine-made papers.

Watermarks, the trademarks of papermakers, began to be incorporated into the mesh of the tray in Italy from the 1250s.

All paper was handmade until 1798, when the Frenchman Nicolas-Louis Robert invented a papermaking machine which made a continuous roll of paper. This was developed and perfected in England as the Fourdrinier machine in 1804.

During the nineteenth century, wood pulp took over from cloth fibre as the basis of the papermaking process. Book production was expanding and there was a shortage of cloth. A process of machine grinding and chemically treating wood pulp was developed in Germany and quickly spread to Northern Europe and America.

Machine-made paper is relatively inexpensive to produce but has a limited shelf-life since it contains acidic chemicals which cause it to deteriorate. Unfortunately, this type of paper is still widely used today.

Modern paper can be coated to give special surfaces – for example china clay paper, used for art books.

Folding

The way the sheets are folded determines the size of the book. The folio, the quarto and the octavo are made when the sheet is folded once, twice and three times respectively. These are often abbreviated to Fo.; Qto or 4to, 4; Oct., 8vo, 8.

A folded sheet (or leaf) is called a section, or a gathering. When a book is open, the right-hand sheet is called the recto, the left-hand sheet (the reverse of the recto), the verso.

Collating

On receiving the sheets of manuscript or printed text, the binder ensures that the sections are in correct order. This is done by collating or checking the signatures, letters found at the tail margin of the sheets at the beginning of each section. Preliminary sheets, including title pages and blank end-papers (which are added by the binder), are not lettered.

Sewing

Stabbing was one of the earliest forms of sewing. Thread is passed through holes pierced in the sheets along the spine edge. Papyrus codices of *single* sheets were attached in this way. Pamphlets comprising few sections (common from the sixteenth to eighteenth centuries) are also stab sewn. 'Japanese sewing' refers to oriental texts sewn through the side and secured by a flat knot.

Coptic bindings containing folded sections of papyrus were often sewn using a type of chain stitch. Thread was passed through the inner folds of each section and linked to the next section at the outside of

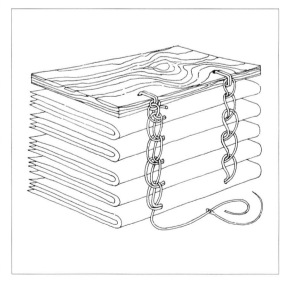

18. Coptic binding with Coptic sewing.

19. A sewing frame.

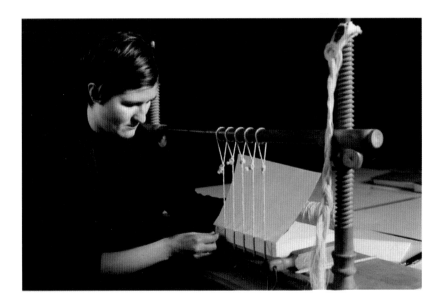

the folds (*see* fig. 18). This sewing style spread from the Mediterranean to north-western Europe. It is not known exactly when the style became widely used, but the earliest-known English binding, the seventh-century Stonyhurst Gospel (*see* fig. 52) is sewn in this way.

Most sewing techniques (except stabbing and Coptic sewing) are carried out on a sewing frame (*see* fig. 19), in use in Europe by the twelfth century and possibly as early as the tenth century. Each section is sewn around the sewing supports and is linked to its neighbouring sections via a kettle stitch (visible in figs. 20–23) made at the top and tail of the outer fold.

Examples of flexible sewing (*see* fig. 20) have been found on bindings from as early as the ninth century. It requires sewing the book around thongs which lie horizontally across the spine of the text block. An especially heavy text block might call for the book to be sewn around double supports, or a piece of leather split into two, or alternate double and single supports.

From the late sixteenth century, cords could be recessed (*see* fig 21); cuts or grooves are made in the backs of the sections to accommodate the thickness of the thong or support. The covered binding features a smooth spine without bands. (False bands could also be added to a book sewn in this way.)

There are a variety of sewing techniques. All-along sewing is one of the most common (*see* fig. 22); the thread is run up and down each

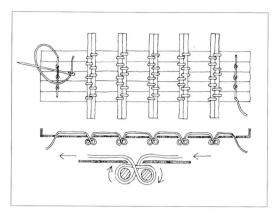

20. (ABOVE) Flexible sewing over double cords.

21. (ABOVE RIGHT) Recessed cord sewing.

22. (RIGHT) All-along sewing on tapes.

23. Decorated papers used as end-leaves or wrappers. Blue paste paper; 'Dutch gilt' embossed floral paper; comb marbled paper; plain blue wrapper on pamphlet BL RB.23.a.393; background block printed paper signed 'Orléans Chez Rabier-Boulard' BL Olga Hirsch collection J1390.

section and around the sewing support without interruption. 'Two-on', a quick method, involves more than one section being sewn on at once.

It is possible to dispense with sewing. In 1836, William Hancock was granted a patent for caoutchouc bindings. Single leaves, not folded sections, were attached along the spine with a rubber solution (caoutchouc is a French term for rubber). The process is known as perfect binding, although it was sometimes called gutta-percha. The term 'perfect' is flattering, as this type of binding does not wear well; spines crack and pages fall out, still a characteristic of modern paper-backs.

End-leaves

End-leaves are plain or decorated folded sheets added by the binder to protect the text from the boards of the binding and to strengthen the structure. They are attached to the text block by tipping in with paste and sewing.

The 'paste-down' (or board-paper) lines the inside of the cover and conceals the raw edges where the covering material turns in around the board. However, in some pre-fifteenth century bindings, this sheet may not have been have been pasted down (or has subsequently become loose) and the turn-in of the covering material is clearly visible.

The 'fly-leaf' is the term given to the free end-paper. Fly-leaves can be pasted together. This can be seen when marbled paper is used for the end-leaves; one side of the sheet (the 'recto') will be marbled, the other side (the 'verso'), acts as a backing sheet and is plain (the 'stiff leaf end-paper').

From the seventeenth century, marbled paper (*see* fig. 23) was frequently used for end-leaves. It seems likely that many binders purchased papers which had already been marbled. Colours were floated on the surface of a bath of size or gum. A design was drawn into the colours using differently shaped implements; a comb-shape was popular. When a sheet of paper was applied to the surface of the bath, the pattern would transfer to the paper. This practice was developed in the East, and examples known as Suminagashi were produced in Japan from about 800 AD. The Persians seem to have been the first to use marbled papers in books (examples are found in sixteenth-century manuscripts) and by the end of the sixteenth century, marbled end-leaves were made in Holland. The English diarist John Evelyn gave a lecture to the Royal Society on the subject in 1662.[44] There are different marbling patterns including Turkish spot (also called stone marbling), Antique Spot, French Curl (also called Snail) and Nonpareil.

Decorated paper was popular throughout eighteenth-century Europe. The most important centres of manufacture were Germany, France and Italy. Some papers can be identified from the manufacturers' names printed on the sheets, as illustrated here (*see* fig. 23).

Patterned blocks of wood or metal were most commonly used to decorate the paper. French manufacturers of wood-block papers were called 'Dominotiers'. Paris, Orléans, Rouen, and Tournai were centres of the trade. 'Cotton papers', also common in France, refer to papers decorated by wood blocks designed for use in the textile printing trade. (Ink impressions made by the small metal pins which were used in the process can sometimes be seen on the paper.)

Germany was famous for producing gold-blocked paper depicting hunting scenes, animals, portraits of saints and other religious themes. 'Dutch gilt' was a multi-coloured floral pattern blocked in gold, which was sent to the Netherlands for re-export.

Paste papers, in use from the sixteenth to the eighteenth centuries, were made by pressing objects (often the craftsman's thumb!) into a mixture of paste and paint. These are often found in blue or red/pink on German bindings and are sometimes referred to as 'Herrnhuter Papier', after the religious community in Herrnhut where paste papers of this type were made.

Doublures
For luxury bindings, cloth (frequently watered silk) or leather is often used to line the inside of the covers, in the place of the paste-down. This is called a 'doublure' (*see* figs 45 and 76). The cloth or leather doublure can be tooled in gold, blind or black ink. Doublures, although not common, were used in Europe from the sixteenth century.

Rounding and backing the spine
Sewing caused the spine to swell. From the early sixteenth century, a technique ('rounding') was employed to counteract the tendency for the spine to be pulled inwards by the weight of the text block. The surface was glued and pulled or hammered to form a convex arc. Later, the shapes of spines varied according to binding fashion.

'Backing', in use from the second quarter of the sixteenth century, helped the spine maintain its shape. The back of each section was hammered over its neighbour from the centre outwards. At the front and back of the text block, the first and last few sections formed a shoulder against which the boards of the binding rested.

Limp bindings

Books sewn on strips of vellum (known as 'slips', *see* fig. 51) or on alum-tawed leather thongs were often simply laced into vellum covers. This was a cheap and easy form of binding and was surprisingly hard-wearing; it was often used for music scores and academic texts (*see* fig. 25). In excessive heat, however, limp vellum covers warped, as the following description indicates: 'The furious heat of the sun, in only a quarter of an hour or so, had had such a powerful effect on the vellum that both covers were completely and tightly curled up like a brace of white brandy-snaps.'[45]

Boards

The earliest boards were made of papyrus. Medieval boards, however, were made of wood. Its weight pressed the sheets flat, particularly necessary in the case of parchment which tended to pucker or cockle. Local wood was used – in medieval Germany and Italy, beech; in England and France, oak. Wood was a useful base on which to attach clasps, metal panels and other 'furniture' (for example bosses).

Initially boards were cut square, but by the fifteenth century edges were often bevelled or shaped to accommodate clasps (*see* fig. 43).

24. A Greek-style binding on *Epistolae Graecae*, Venice, 1499 by Claude Picques for Markus Fugger. Note the double endband, the high head caps, grooved boards, and clasps of plaited thongs and pins (the tail-edge clasp is missing).
BL Davis 379.

Greek-style binding (popular in the Mediterranean in the fifteenth and sixteenth centuries) involved sticking together two sheets of wood so that, when covered by leather, a groove was formed (*see* fig. 24).

Pasteboards began to replace wooden boards in the sixteenth century. They were made by pasting together sheets of paper until the required thickness was achieved. With the advent of paper, heavy boards were no longer needed. However, wooden boards continued in use (particularly in Germany) until the nineteenth century. Thin wood ('scabboard') was used for cheap

books bought ready-bound, particularly in seventeenth-century America.

Boards were sometimes made of other materials, including papier-mâché, which was used in the nineteenth century to satisfy the taste for novelty bindings. Bindings with covers which resemble carved wood were made from papier-mâché, sometimes moulded around a metal frame.

25. G M Crespi, *Rayon de bibliothèque*, c.1717–15, depicting vellum bindings. Note the limp vellum binding with the curled cover.
Photograph courtesy of the Conservatorio di Musica G B Martini, Bologna.

26. Lacing in.

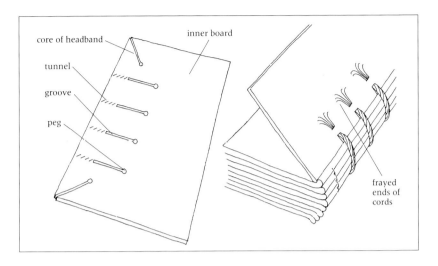

Attaching the text block to the boards

This was often allied to the sewing process. Coptic sewing involved the thread being passed directly through pre-bored holes in the boards (*see* fig. 18). In early raised thong sewing, the thongs were channelled through pre-bored grooves or tunnels and secured by a wooden peg. This procedure was called 'lacing in' and there were many different methods. When the use of wood declined, holes were pierced in the pasteboards through which cords or other sewing supports were threaded (*see* fig. 26).

There are several types of joint (the area where the board meets the spine) and their use varies. Split boards require a French groove (or joint), where the boards are set a little way from the spine allowing more space for the book to open, placing the pressure on the covering material (*see* fig. 27). A closed (or tight) joint occurred when the boards abutted the backing shoulders of the text block.

27. A french groove.

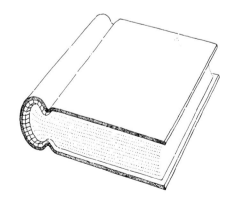

Edge trimming

Text blocks are composed of folded sheets, so the folds have to be cut before every page of the bound book can be turned. The folded edges are called 'bolts'. Simple methods include cutting with shears, or a knife and rule, either before or after sewing. The edges can be planed for extra smoothness.

The pages of Islamic bindings were always cut even with the covers, unlike western bindings which were cut smaller than the covers, leaving margins called 'squares'.

By the sixteenth century, a 'plough' was in use comprising a cutting blade held between two blocks of wood. It was drawn along the edges of the leaves whilst the text block was held firmly in a lying press (a small horizontal bench-top press used for clamping books – *see* fig. 32).

The guillotine, developed for use in bookbinding in the 1830s, was also used for edge trimming. It was particularly useful for bindings where the edges of the leaves had to be cut flush with the covers, as with modern paperbacks.

Edge decoration

Until around the sixteenth century, books were stored so that the edges were visible. Details of author and title were frequently written in ink on the edges of the text block when the book was closed.

Edges were also decorated with colour, a practice known in the fourth century and sometimes still carried out today. Watercolour is brushed or sprinkled on to the edges. Marbled colours can also be applied. (*See* fig. 43 for painted edges.)

Initially, designs were abstract, simple shapes like diamonds, leaves and scrollwork. From the 1300s, more elaborate designs, often incorporating coats of arms and religious motifs, appeared. These paintings were visible when the book was closed.

From the middle of the seventeenth century, some fore-edges were painted so that the designs were visible only when the pages were fanned out. The text block was held in a press so that only a minute section of the upper surface of each printed page was revealed, and paint was applied to this area (rather than the edge of the page) which was then gilt (covered with gold leaf). Edwards of Halifax bindings were famous for this in eighteenth-century England.

From the beginning of the twentieth century, fore-edges came to be collected in their own right, which encouraged a market for forgeries. It is difficult to tell if a painting is contemporary with the text. The paintings are sometimes signed with a name or initials but one cannot always be sure if the name refers to the artist, or to the binder.

Gilding was (and is) the most common form of edge decoration. It seems to have originated in Italy in the 1460s, evolving alongside the

28. Painted, gilt and gauffered fore-edge of *Biblia*, Wittenberg, 1575 depicting the arms of Hans Harrer. BL Davis 692.

gold-tooling technique. Size, a mixture which often included white of egg and water was applied to the leaves of the sewn book which had been cut smooth. (If the edges were gilded *before* sewing, the gold surface appeared irregular, and was known as 'rough gilt'.) Gold leaf was applied and then burnished. The resulting thin layer protected the text from dust.

Gauffering, the application of warmed binding tools to gilded edges, developed towards the end of the fifteenth century. Patterns were frequently built up by repeated impressions of dots (*see* fig. 28).

Before the sixteenth century, some manuscripts had small leather tabs which protruded from the fore-edges. These were used to divide the text (as with modern file dividers).

Endbands
An endband is a decorative band at the head and tail of a book which protects the spine edges of the text block (*see* fig. 29). It is made by

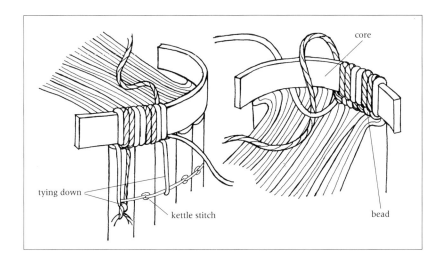

29. Headbands.

working linen or silk threads over a core of leather, rolled paper, strips of vellum or cane. The earliest examples were probably undyed (*see* fig. 43); later, bands were worked with stripes of different colours.

In some twelfth-century bindings, the endband was incorporated into the main sewing process. By the sixteenth century, endbands were worked independently and anchored by tying them down under the kettle stitch (the first and last rows of stitching which secure each section to its neighbour).

From the sixteenth century onwards, the endband with a single core, worked in linen thread (and later, coloured silks) and featuring a row of beading, became the most common type, although continental binders have also favoured double bands.

The format of endbands varies with the style of the binding; for example, Greek-style bindings (*see* fig. 24) had double bands worked in red and blue, and some late fifteenth-century German bindings had plaited endbands (*see* fig. 43).

Towards the end of the sixteenth century (and earlier in Germany), a purely decorative stuck-on endband emerged. This was not sewn down into the backs of the sections. Machine-made versions have been in use since the nineteenth century.

Lining and backing

Bindings from the twelfth and thirteenth centuries indicate that at that time there was no attempt to stick the covering material to the spine. Later practices varied. Sometimes, strips of waste parchment (frequently recycled manuscripts) or paper were pasted to the back of the sections.

The term 'tight back' describes a binding where the covering material is stuck on to the backs of the sections, either directly or to a layer (a 'strengthener') sandwiched between the spine and cover (*see* fig. 30). The use of the tight back was common until the eighteenth

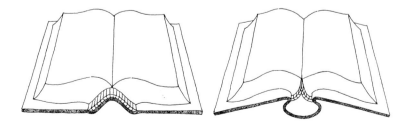

30. Tight and hollow backs.

century in France and slightly later (*c.*1800) in England. In the late nineteenth century, the tight back was revived for fine bindings by the English craft binder T.J. Cobden-Sanderson, but was not taken up by the trade in general.

The term 'hollow back' describes a binding where the covering material is not stuck directly to the back of the sections (*see* fig. 30). The method was developed in France in the second half of the eighteenth century, but was rare in England until the 1820s. The cords onto which the text block was sewn were recessed into grooves cut into the backs of the sections, and a paper tube (a 'hollow') was used as a liner between the sections and spine covering. Techniques varied for making the hollow, but the quality of the paper was poor (except for fine bindings), often composed of waste printed matter.

Covering materials

The book can be covered in various ways with various materials – leather, cloth, paper or a combination of those elements. The most common styles are 'full bound' where the whole binding (i.e. boards and spine) is completely covered; 'half bound', where just the spine and corners are covered; and 'quarter bound', where only the spine is covered.

In the area encompassing Germany, Hungary, Slovakia and the Netherlands, a second protective covering was sometimes placed over the first decorated covers of the boards. This was known as a *Hülleneinband* and examples can be found on manuscripts of the fifteenth century and earlier.

Leather: Leather is an animal skin which has been tanned, that is, soaked in tannin (derived from plant or vegetable material). Animal skins are naturally flexible but the hair must be removed and the surface smoothed.

Early Coptic bindings were sometimes covered with tanned leather, as were seventh- and eighth-century English bindings. However, it was from the fifteenth century that tanned leather became the norm.

According to some authorities, a skin which has not been tanned cannot strictly be called leather. From the twelfth to the early fifteenth century, whittawing (or tawing) involved the immersion of goat, pig or sheepskin in a solution of alum and salts. This turned the skin white, soft and flexible (fig. 41 shows alum-tawed pigskin).

Vellum or parchment, in use as a covering material from at least as early as the fourteenth century, was made from skins which were not tanned but soaked in lime, de-haired and dried under tension.

Types of leather: Each country tended to use the skin from indigenous animals. In the fifteenth century, binders in Germany commonly used pigskin; in England, calfskin and in Italy, goatskin. Throughout the Islamic world, goatskin and sheepskin were used. As the surface of leather bindings deteriorates, it can be difficult to determine what type of skin was used. There are, however, certain pointers:

Calfskin: Calfskin is soft and smooth with little veining. As a calf ages, its skin, or hide, becomes tougher and more lined. Calfskin provides a good base for both blind-tooled decoration (that is, when heated tools make an impression into the leather) and gold-tooling (when gold leaf is added to the impression). Its smoothness makes it susceptible to scratches and scuffing, but it is nevertheless sturdy. It was in use from as early as the twelfth century (*see* fig. 33 for a calfskin binding).

Calf skins are sometimes inverted so that the inner side is uppermost, giving the binding the appearance of suede. This is called reversed calf.

'Russia' or Russia calf bindings were popular between 1780 and 1830. The process involved tanning and treating the calfskin with aromatic birch bark oil. The leather was often dyed a reddish brown and diced (giving a pattern of latticed lines). It was, however, difficult to handle and tended to rot; it seems that the specially-treated Russia calf could not withstand the effects of pollution caused by gas-lighting.

Goatskin: Goatskin has a definite grain; its surface is irregular with furrows, ridges and hair follicles. It is spongy to the touch, although it can dry out and harden with age. It seems likely that the Moors first produced alum-tawed goatskin before the eleventh century, but it was *tanned* goatskin which became common in Europe from around the middle of the sixteenth-century (and earlier in Italy and Spain) to the present time. Goatskin was imported into Europe through Turkey and Venice. Indeed, the goatskin used in seventeenth-century England was called Turkey (*see* fig. 6), although it later became known as Morocco. (Confusingly, the term 'Morocco' is sometimes used to describe all goatskin.) Other skins were supplied from Africa and have related names such as Levant, Niger, and Oasis.

Goatskin takes dye very well and bindings are often richly coloured with red, blue and green. Gold-tooling is the usual and most effective form of decoration on goatskin. (*See* figs 45 and 76 for examples of goatskin.)

Pigskin: Pigskin can be recognised by the arrangement of the hair follicles in triangular groups of three, interconnected by a criss-cross pattern of graining. Pigskin was usually alum-tawed (*see above*) which made the surface white. Pigskin bindings were most popular in Germany from around 1550–1640 on books with wooden boards. Although frequently blind-tooled, the heated tools did not darken the skin, so the pattern on pigskin bindings was sometimes indistinct. (*See* fig. 41 for a pigskin binding.)

Sheepskin: The characteristic arrangement of follicles on sheepskin reflects the curly wool of sheep. The surface is slightly spongy to the touch. It is not a robust material and, when damaged, peels away in strips and is easily scuffed. Tawing can make the skin more durable; there are examples of alum-tawed sheepskin bindings dating from the fourteenth century.

Sheepskin was very cheap and often used for the lower end of the market where books were sold ready-bound. However, the surface was often treated to make it resemble a more expensive skin.

Roan, popular from around 1790 as a cheap substitute for goatskin, and skiver, commonly used for lettering pieces on the spines of books, were both derived from split sheepskin treated with sumach (a vegetable tanning material).

Vellum or parchment: Vellum or parchment (any skin treated with lime and dried under tension) is strong, light and cheap. The surface is hard, smooth and generally white, although it can be stained any colour. However, it shrinks when wet, and warps when exposed to heat. (*See* figs 25 and 51 for vellum bindings.)

Although it was in use much earlier, vellum is often found on sixteenth- and seventeenth-century texts which were sold ready bound. Vellum subsequently enjoyed a revival in the nineteenth century on books produced by private presses.

The edges of the limp vellum covers were sometimes turned over the text, making a protective flap over the fore-edge. 'Yapp edges' is the term given when the vellum is turned over all three edges.

Vellum bindings were sometimes pierced and cut away to reveal an underlying layer of coloured silks. Leather bindings could be similarly pierced.

Other animal skins: The skins of many other animals have been used as covering for bindings, including crocodileskin, sealskin, snakeskin, and sharkskin. Deerskin (sometimes called buckskin or doeskin), used in conjunction with wooden boards, is often described as being commonly used from the eighth to the fifteenth centuries. (These descriptions must be treated with caution, however, since old and worn deerskin is difficult to distinguish from other skins.) It was often alum-tawed rather than tanned and the bindings were white, although occasionally dyed red. Deerskin bindings feel soft and have the appearance of suede.

Artificial graining of skin: The artificial graining of skin, invented in England at the end of the eighteenth century, was achieved by impressing wooden or metal plates cut with a pattern on to the leather. Cheaper skins like sheepskin were grained to look like expensive goatskin. (From the nineteenth century the surface of cloth was also grained – *see* page 46, below.)

Cloth: Cloth, including velvet, satin and embroidered canvas, was considered appropriate for luxury bindings. Cloth (and sometimes soft leather) was used for chemise bindings, dating from the twelfth to fifteenth centuries. The material, cut considerably larger than the bound book, was stitched around the wooden boards, and the overlapping fabric was wrapped around to protect it.

Plain canvas (usually buff-coloured and coarsely textured) was used for cheap books bought ready-bound, such as school text books.

The structure remained basically the same as for leather bindings until around 1823 when case binding in cloth appeared. This was a manufacturing process developed to meet the needs of publishers for whole editions of their work bound uniformly and cheaply. Cloth cases incorporating covers and spines were made up separately from the text block and attached later.

The 1820s saw new book cloths for publishers' bindings. At first, plain cloth was used but by the 1830s, techniques were invented to enhance the appearance of the bindings. Graining machines produced a variety of finishes including ribbed or 'T' grain, sand, diaper (cross hatched with diamond shapes), bead and pebble grain. Surfaces were also embossed. Buckram, popular today for re-binding books in libraries, did not become widely used until around 1880.

Paper: Paper covers are not new – they were used in Italy and Germany towards the end of the fifteenth century. Paper was a cheap and easy material for binders to use but it was not hard-wearing. The paper could be plain or decorated. It was suitable for binding pamphlets or small books comprising few sections, for example music scores.

A paper wrapper was often considered to be a temporary covering. When collectors bought a text, they could choose to have it bound according to their own requirements.

With the introduction of edition binding in the nineteenth century, paper was sometimes used to cover the boards instead of cloth. This is described as 'paper boards'.

Other covering materials: Tortoise-shell was used for luxury bindings in the seventeenth century, often combined with silver fittings. In the nineteenth century there was a fashion for novelty bindings. Covers were made from ivory, imitation ivory, papier-mâché, mother of pearl, and even cork and fur!

Methods of covering

The covering material was measured against the spine and boards of the open book and cut so that there was an overlap which could be turned in around the boards. Paste made from wheat flour was used to attach the cover. As it dried slowly, it gave the binder time to complete even difficult operations.

Religious texts were sometimes given 'treasure bindings' made of precious metals. These books were not covered in the traditional sense but were inserted into the metal covers (which had been made by metalworkers or jewellers).

In the case of leather, it was necessary to pare or thin the skin, especially around the edges and spine. Binders today use a spoke-shave, but in the past it is likely that binders bought leather at the

31. Qur'an (pt 25). Arabic
manuscript (late fourteenth
century). Egyptian binding
with flap.
BL Davis 701.

appropriate thickness from the manufacturer, or paid a currier (a professional leatherworker) to thin the skins, since the work required a
skilled hand. They would have completed the operation themselves
with a paring knife.

The lower covers of leather bindings in countries influenced by
Islamic traditions (Spain, Persia, and Turkey) were extended into flaps
which projected over the fore-edge (*see* fig 31). Spines were always
smooth.

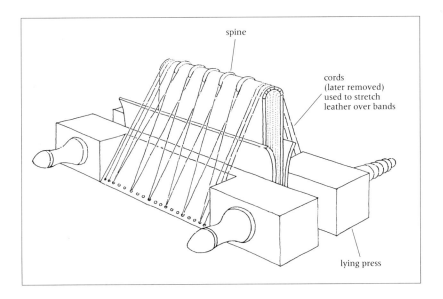

labels: spine; cords (later removed) used to stretch leather over bands; lying press

32. Tying up.

In the Middle Ages, the fabric of chemise bindings was formed into a pocket into which the boards were slotted. Sometimes the fabric was riveted in place by bosses nailed through into the boards. Alternatively, the fabric was secured by sewing the ends together at the corner turn-ins.

With the later use of cloth, the material was applied to the binding in the same way as with leather. Thin or delicate fabrics like satin and silk were sometimes lined with paper for added strength before covering took place.

Headcaps
Twelfth-century bindings often feature a tab of semi-circular leather at the top of the spine to strengthen it. It could be sewn round with a whip stitch in coloured threads and was lined with coloured cloth. From the thirteenth century, the tab was replaced by a simpler form; the leather was cut so that it just covered the headband. By the sixteenth century, the leather was often turned inwards over the spine to protect the top and tail edges. This was called a headcap and it has continued in use to the present. Greek-style bindings have high headcaps (*see* fig. 24).

Tying up
From the thirteenth century, the process known as 'tying up' was

introduced. It was particularly appropriate for use with sewing on raised supports and for boards attached with a groove along the spine edge (*see* fig. 32). Often the mark of the cords can be seen as v-shaped indentations on the spine edge of the covers of a binding. Tying up became less common with the decline of sewing on raised supports in the early nineteenth century. Binders today use pincers called band nippers to achieve the same effect.

Furniture and fittings

Fittings added to bindings look decorative, but also have an important function:

Fastenings: Clasps put pressure on the wooden boards which kept the parchment leaves flat. They were made to fit the individual book and nailed or riveted to the boards either before or after decoration had been applied to the cover. (Figs 24, 33, 43, 70 feature clasps.)

33. Empty covers of a Netherlandish calfskin binding with clasps and cornerpieces, 1500. BL Davis 683.

Clasps were made of iron, brass or precious metals and came in a variety of designs. They were frequently elaborately shaped and engraved, often with a religious phrase or name.

In the fifteenth/sixteenth centuries, clasps on English and French bindings were attached to the upper cover and caught on to the lower cover, whereas on German and Netherlandish bindings the method was reversed so that when the book was open, the clasp protruded from the lower board. In Italy, four clasps were common, two over the fore-edge and one each over the top and tail edges. Greek-style bindings featured plaited thongs catching onto metal pins protruding from the edge of the board (*see* fig. 24).

Substantial clasps became less common with the introduction of pasteboards. Bibles and prayer books traditionally had clasps (often silver, as in fig. 70), whatever the size or date of the binding.

Ties (commonly used in conjunction with pasteboards or limp vellum) were made of leather, linen or silk and often appeared in pairs attached through holes near the fore-edges of the covers. They were used to prevent the covers from warping. Often the fabric of the ties has worn away, leaving just the holes, as in fig. 62. Ties were especially popular for use on charters or grants as they dignified the appearance of the binding (*see* figs 47, 65).

Other fittings: Bosses and metal corner and centrepieces protected the covering material and decoration from wear. This was especially important when books were stored flat, not standing upright, as is the practice today. Bosses also helped secure the covering material, particularly fabric, to the wooden boards (*see* fig. 43).

Protective pieces of metal ('shoes', *see* fig. 43) were sometimes nailed to the edge of the boards near the top and tail of the spine.

Book marks (or 'registers') made of coloured silk or cord are often found in religious works. The marker ran under the headband and was glued to the spine.

Parchment lettering pieces with manuscript details of author and title were sometimes affixed to the upper cover of a book. A protective layer of translucent horn was placed over the parchment and nailed into the wooden board.

In medieval libraries, books were kept chained up as a security measure. A metal ring was riveted to the wooden board of the binding to which a chain was attached. The chains could be as long as five feet and were fitted with a swivel to prevent the links from twisting.

Finishing

Decorative techniques

Tooling

Tooling, in use from the fifth century until the present day, is a common form of decoration. Tools were (and are) used on leather and vellum bindings; velvet was sometimes tooled but this was uncommon. Paper was occasionally tooled.

'Blind-tooling' involves the pressing of heated tools into leather, which slightly darkens the surface of the skin (*see* fig. 33 for a clear example).

'Gold-tooling' involves the pressing of the tools through gold leaf (fig. 65 is a clear example). 'Glaire', a mixture of egg white and vinegar, helps it to adhere. The technique of gold-tooling, known in the Islamic world since the thirteenth century, reached Europe in the middle of the fifteenth century.

Tools are made of engraved brass dies held in wooden handles. A fillet makes a continuous straight line; a roll (a wheel shape) creates a continuous strip of decoration (*see* fig. 66), and individual tools (*see* figs 34–36) make single motifs. Blocks are slightly larger and are often used to form corner or centrepieces. Arms blocks which impress coats of arms (*see* figs 6, 8, 12, 68), were usually lent to the binder by the commissioning family, although binders sometimes made up the design with individual hand stamps from their own workshops.

Individual tools are cut to many designs – flowers, foliage, and animals. Tools can be solid (*see* fig. 34): 'pointillé', where the outline is a broken line composed of dots (*see* fig. 35): 'azured' or 'hatched' where the design comprises parallel diagonal lines (*see* fig. 36).

34. Bull motif gold-tooled on binding of *Missale Romanum*, Antwerp, 1663. BL C.66.i.3.

35. Flower motif made by pointillé tool on the binding of Marin Cureau de la Chambre, *Les Characteres de Passions*, III, Paris, 1568. BL Davis 523.

36. Azured motifs gold-tooled on binding of Lucian [Works], Venice, 1522. BL C.19.g.7.

By the seventeenth century, details of author and title were frequently tooled onto the spine, either directly onto the leather or using a separate lettering piece. Earlier, this had not been necessary, as books were either shelved upright with the fore-edge (not the spine) showing or were laid flat in chests or on lecterns. Words were either written in ink on the fore-edge or bottom edge of the text block or a parchment slip with manuscript notes was pasted to the cover. T. Kimball Brooker (*see* Further Reading) has examined the subject of lettered fore-edges and the storage of books in detail, with special reference to sixteenth-century Italian texts.

Identifying bindings by tools

The date or place of publication of the text is not a reliable guide to the date or place of the binding because most books were not sold ready-bound. It was common for printed sheets to be sent to different towns and countries (often exported inside barrels for protection) and bound up if and when the customer required it.

Before the sixteenth century, binders cannot often be identified by their real names. Later researchers have given them names taken from the distinctive tools they used, hence the Oxford fifteenth-century Fishtail binder (*see* fig. 37). In some areas, however, there was a local tradition of 'signing' a binding with the workman's name; at least twenty-one binders in fifteenth-century Erfurt used name stamps.

Initials found on panel stamps (*see below*) and rolls sometimes belong to the binder, but may also refer to the publisher, bookseller, artist or engraver of the tools.

Bindings can be attributed by identifying the tools used in a particular workshop, although the similarity of tools can cause problems. A precise identification is easier when a tool has a distinguishing feature, for example, if it is damaged (*see* fig. 38).

37. Fish tailed monster motif blind-tooled on the binding of *Cato moralissimus,* Deventer, [12 Mar 1492 – 6 Jun 1500] by the Fishtail Binder. IA 4755.

From the eighteenth century, binders commonly 'signed' their work by tooling or ink-stamping their names on or inside the binding. Alternatively, a binder's ticket, a paper label printed with the binder's name and address, was pasted to the end-leaves (*see* fig. 39). (It is unwise to attribute a binding on the strength of a binder's ticket alone, since labels are sometimes soaked off and transferred.) Signatures can be found in various places; at the bottom of spines (*see* fig. 74), on turn-ins, on upper covers (*see* fig 53b), end-leaves or (less commonly) on painted fore-edges.

Certain motifs proliferated throughout Europe and can be misinterpreted; a crown motif does not always denote royal ownership, the initials IHS do not invariably indicate a Jesuit provenance (*see* fig. 15, which has no Jesuit connection), a fleur-de-lys need not indicate a

38. Damaged greek key design roll (enlarged) on the binding of *The Castle of Otranto,* Parma, 1791 by Edwards of Halifax. BL C.154.i.20.

39. (RIGHT) The binder's ticket of the Parisian nineteenth-century binder, Tessier, on Evariste Forges de Parny, *Les Rosecroix*, Paris, 1807.
BL C.150.k.15.

40. (FAR RIGHT) Double-headed eagle motif blind-tooled on the binding of John Lathbury, *Liber morialium*, [Oxford], 1482 by the Rood and Hunt Bindery in Oxford.
BL IB 55317a.

French binding (*see* fig. 60, an Italian binding), a double-headed eagle is neither exclusively Habsburg nor German (*see* fig. 40).

Panel stamps

Panel stamps, which may have been cast rather than engraved, are large tools incorporating a complete design, and were applied to the moistened leather covers of a binding by means of a press. In a large book, several panels were used to cover the whole area. The earliest known panel stamp was made in Antwerp in the thirteenth century, but use flourished in England, France and the Netherlands in the fifteenth and sixteenth centuries, and in Germany into the seventeenth century. Designs, sometimes copied from woodcut illustrations, included biblical scenes, allegorical figures, coats of arms, acorns, and portraits of princes (*see* fig. 41) and religious reformers.

Gold or blind blocking was the nineteenth-century equivalent of panel stamping. A blocking press was used to stamp designs in gold, blind or ink on to leather covers or the cloth cases of publisher's bindings. An embossing press (*see* fig. 42), used for machine-made bindings, blocked a complete design (covers and spine) on a case before it was attached to the text block. Douglas Leighton has written that 'a fly embossing press, surely one of the strangest monsters that have ever been introduced to the trade, was a necessary machine to every binder of consequence... I well remember its appearance in the dim light of a basement, a massive ungainly frame of iron surmounted by a dumb-bell of the kind that comes to a circus strong man only in his very bad dreams.'[46] The leather or cloth was embossed using metal dies and a heat process. Embossed bindings on Bibles and devotional works were popular in England, France and Germany.

Cut leather work

Cut leather work (also known as Lederschnitt and cuir ciselé) was used from the end of fourteenth to beginning of the sixteenth centuries, particularly in Germany (*see* fig. 43). A design was incised into dampened leather using a knife. Punches were sometimes used to depress the background, throwing the design into relief.

Onlays and inlays

Onlays are materials which have been pasted onto the surface covering of a binding (*see* figs 6, 15, 45, 53b, 76, & 79). In theory, any material can be onlaid, but thinly-pared coloured leathers were often chosen. Less commonly, materials can also be 'inlaid'; the covering leather is cut away and a contrasting material is inset (*see* fig. 46). These are relatively inexpensive methods of decoration (and certainly cheaper than buying binding tools!).

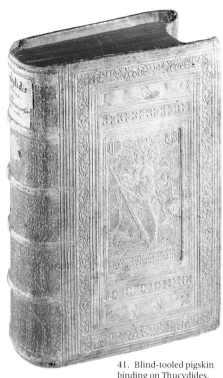

41. Blind-tooled pigskin binding on Thucydides, *Historiae de bello Peloponnesiaco*, Wittenberg, 1580 featuring a panel stamp depicting the Holy Roman Emperor, Charles V.
BL Davis 631.

42. A nineteenth-century English embossing press from Charles Tomlinson, (ed.), *Cyclopaedia of Useful Arts*, London, 1866, I, p.155.
BL 8765.e.25.

Treasure bindings

In medieval churches, religious books were sometimes richly bound and decorated with gold, silver, ivory, coloured enamels and jewels (*see* fig. 44). These bindings were produced by metalworkers, jewellers and craftsmen other than bookbinders. Silver or elaborately-carved ivory plaques did not form part of the structure of the book but were made separately and then nailed onto the wooden boards of a binding. These plaques were often transferred from book to book as texts wore out.

There were also decorated metal slipcases or boxes into which any text of the appropriate size could be inserted. In Ireland from the ninth to the twelfth centuries, there was a tradition for holy books to be kept in a Cumdach (a metal slipcase or box). Sometimes the books were taken into battle, protected by the Cumdach, which hung round a warrior's neck and served as a breastplate. This type of slipcase or box was also used in Scotland.

Small editions of the Qur'an were housed in jewelled or enamelled boxes or in fabric satchels.

Tiny books decorated with gilt, enamel or jewels were sometimes worn on cords or chains. Examples can be seen in court portraits of sixteenth-century England.

43. (BELOW) A cut leather binding on *Petri Comestoris Histora Scholastica*. MS, fifteenth century. Note the shaped boards, 2 clasps catching onto the upper cover, metal shoes, 5 bosses, plaited endband and painted fore-edge. BL Add Ms 18972.

44. (BELOW LEFT) Treasure binding, on *Homiliae variae*, MS., twelfth to thirteenth century, decorated with gilt metal plates, champlevé enamel, semi-precious stones, antique cameos and rock crystals. Photograph courtesy of the Bodleian Library, University of Oxford.

Jewelled bindings

Jewels frequently adorned treasure bindings and the taste was revived in late nineteenth- and early twentieth-century England. Perhaps the most famous jewelled binding of that time was on a copy of *The Rubaiyat of Omar Khayyam* (1884) bound by Francis Sangorski of the Sangorski and Sutcliffe bindery in 1909. 1050 jewels including topazes, turquoises, rubies and garnets were incorporated into the design. The binding had an unlucky history. The first version was lost with the sinking of the Titanic in 1912. A second version, re-created in 1939 by Sutcliffe's nephew, Stanley Bray, was damaged in the blitz. Undaunted by this, Mr Bray completed a third version (*see* fig. 45) using the salvaged jewels and the resulting volume was placed on indefinite loan in the British Library in 1989.

Decorative cloth

Cloth was frequently the choice for luxury bindings. Queen Elizabeth I favoured velvet bindings in her own library. Paul Hentzner on a visit

45. Upper flyleaf and doublure of *The Rubaiyat of Omar Khayyam*, Boston [Mass.] & London, [1884] bound by Stanley Bray. Mrs Stanley Bray, on loan to BL, C.170.f.10.

to the Royal Library in 1598, noted that the books were all 'bound in velvet of different colours, though chiefly red, with clasps of gold and silver; some have pearls, and precious stones, set in their bindings.'[47] A rather worn example of a binding from Elizabeth's library can be found in the British Library (BL 168.i.30). Cloth was sometimes incorporated into leather bindings too, where it was used to line sunken panels (usually velvet) or to provide a contrasting background for pierced leather covers.

Velvet, satin, silk and canvas bindings were often decorated with embroidery silks, metal threads, pearls and sequins. This form of decoration is not restricted to a particular time or country, but many were produced on prayer books in late sixteenth- and seventeenth-century England (*see* fig. 47). Noblewomen sometimes embroidered the covers themselves, but it seems likely that these bindings were more frequently sewn by professional needleworkers. Appliqué and stumpwork (where the embroidery was raised proud of the cover) were used to depict coats of arms, religious subjects, and rural scenes. The same colours and subjects are found on contemporary clothing and curtains. Ribbon markers, ties made of coloured fabric and painted fore-edges were other embellishments which emphasised the wealth and taste of the owners.

Fabric bindings were sometimes hand-painted or printed and then coloured. The nineteenth-century Parisian binder, Le Fuel, had a thriving trade in binding almanacs and other gift books in printed and painted silk (*see* fig. 53a).

The poet Robert Southey had his 'books of lesser value, which had become ragged and dirty, covered, or rather bound, in coloured cotton prints, for the sake of making them clean and respectable in their appearance, it being impossible to afford the cost of having so many [*c*.1200–1400] put into better bindings.'[48] This was a cheap and easy form of binding since Southey's daughters and any female visitors were given the task of re-covering the books with chintz!

Paints, inks and chemicals
Paint (traditionally water-colour) was a quick and easy way to give a luxury finish to a binding, but in the long term, the pigment sometimes faded and cracked. The black interlace in fig. 64b has been painted.

Paint was most often used on leather or vellum, although it sometimes appeared on cloth, paper and wood, as with the 'tavolette',

46. (OPPOSITE) A French inlaid binding on Alonso Chacon, *Historia utriusque Dacici a Traiano Caesare gesti*, Rome, 1616. BL C.14.c.12.

47. A seventeenth-century English embroidered binding on *The Whole Book of the Psalmes*, London, 1640.
BL C.143.a.10.

painted wooden covers used to protect treasury records in Siena from the thirteenth century (*see* fig. 48).

Painted pictures on various materials, including vellum or ivory, could also be incorporated into leather bindings (*see* fig. 53b). Painted coats of arms covered by a protective sheet of mica were inlaid into French mosaic bindings and a feature of early twentieth-century English 'Cosway' bindings (*see* fig. 10) was their inset miniature paintings (often portraits).

Painted bindings were sometimes given a protective coating, as with the lacquered pictorial bindings of sixteenth- and seventeenth-century Persia (*see* fig. 49), and many of the eastern-influenced Venetian 'ducali' bindings (*see* fig. 62), covering official edicts issued in the name of the Doge (from the fifteenth to eighteenth centuries).

Designs from wood blocks featured on paper bindings from as early as the late fifteenth century in Italy and Germany and are particularly associated with Augsburg, Venice and Ferrara.

Paints, inks and chemicals were sometimes marbled or sprinkled onto the covers (*see* fig. 50), or used with stencils. Recipes in trade manuals show that binders often prepared their own colours, using such ingredients as green copperas, vinegar, potash, walnut shells, and saffron. If the colour contained a high percentage of acid (often the case with black inks), the leather would eventually deteriorate, causing a mottling effect. 'Tree calf' was common from the middle of

48. A painted wooden panel by Guidocci Cozarelli, Siena, 1488. BL Davis 788.

49. Lower cover of a
nineteenth-century Persian
painted and lacquered
binding.
BL Davis 719.

the eighteenth century until the end of the nineteenth century. It was
achieved by chemical treatment of the leather which caused a decorative effect resembling the branches of a tree.

In eighteenth century England, pictures were drawn freehand in
pen and ink onto calf bindings. In the nineteenth century, transfer
processes were used in England and France which 'printed' designs
onto calf or vellum, subsequently to be hand-coloured. Engraved
copper plates could also be used to produce this effect. Early book
cloths were sometimes also printed in inks.

Vellum, naturally a dull white, provided a good base for colour. The easiest method of decoration was to stain the skin, commonly green or red. In the eighteenth century, landscapes were painted directly onto vellum covers. The bindery associated with the firm of Edwards of Halifax produced translucent vellum bindings where designs were painted on to the underside of the skin, thus protecting the picture (*see* fig. 51). The process was patented in 1785. Images were taken from coats of arms or copied from engravings or famous pictures of the day. 'Vellucent' bindings made by Cedric Chivers of Bath from 1903 incorporated a similar technique.

Moulded (or modelled) leather

Leather could also be moulded over shaped boards. Tanned leather was quite easy to shape, providing it had been soaked in water. An example of moulded leather is provided by the earliest surviving decorated European binding, the seventh- or eighth-century Stonyhurst Gospel (*see* fig. 52) which comes from Northumbria. A design worked

50. (BELOW LEFT) Philipp von Stosch, *Gemmae antiquae caelatae sculptorum nominibus insignitae*, Amsterdam, 1724 bound by Joseph Bona. The calf has been sprinked to give a mottled effect. BL C.46.l.5.

51. (BELOW) Lower cover of *The Book of Common Prayer*, Cambridge, 1762 [and] *The Whole Book of Psalms*, Birmingham, 1762 bound in translucent vellum by Edwards of Halifax. BL Davis 210.

in cord and another unidentified material was laid on the surface of the boards. The covering leather was moulded around the cord, so the resulting pattern was raised.

Moulded leather bindings became popular towards the end of the nineteenth century and many were made by women binders. The method was simple and inexpensive. The same technique was also used for screens and boxes.

Binders today mould leather round sculpted boards, producing unusually shaped covers.

Decorative styles

Most books on the subject of decorative binding styles are divided chronologically or nationally, but binding designs were rarely exclusive to a single period or country. An interlacing ribbon pattern can be traced throughout binding history, from eighth-century Egyptian bindings to those of today (interlaces feature in figs 24, 46, 58, 64). The case is similar with corner and centrepiece designs (*see* figs 12, 31, 62), all-over patterns and easily executed panel designs. The mandorla

52 (OPPOSITE) The St Cuthbert Gospel of St John. MS, end of the seventh century. Brown goatskin, incised, painted and moulded to form a raised design.
Stonyhurst College, on loan to BL.

53. Bindings on gift books.
a) Block printed paper binding on *Diario Ecclesiastico*, Lisbon, 1813, BL Hirsch Collection BJ1a.
b) German straw binding on *Tägliches Lob- und Danck-Opfer... in Geistlichen Liedern*, Jena, n.d., BL Davis 647.
c) Spanish mosaic binding on *Estado militar de España*, 1783, by Gabriel de Sancha with painting under mica and binder's signature at tail edge, BL Davis 660.
d) French printed satin binding on *Almanach dédié aux dames pour l'an 1815*, Paris, [1815] by Le Fuel, BL C.183.a.42.

a)   b)   c)   d)

(*see* figs 49 and 62), a popular almond-shaped motif on early Turkish and Persian bindings, was picked up by Venetian binders in the fifteenth century, French and English binders in the sixteenth century and remains in use.

Whatever the country or period, ready markets existed for presentation and prize bindings, miniature 'gift' bindings found on almanacs (*see* figs 53a & d), and armorial bindings (*see* figs 8, 12, 68), whether gold-tooled on leather or worked in embroidery threads.

However, basic styles were open to interpretation. National trends did develop, although describing them is fraught with difficulties. Countries such as Germany, Italy and the Netherlands did not exist as they do now and the boundaries constantly shifted as countries battled for supremacy. The case of the Netherlands exemplifies the problems involved. 'Netherlandish' is used in binding literature to cover regions which may, at one time or another, have been separate countries. The term can embrace Holland, Flanders, and Belgium. The Netherlands was influenced by Spain, which ruled certain northern provinces in the sixteenth and seventeenth centuries, and also by neighbouring Germany and France. However, the Netherlands made its own impact on Europe. There are late fifteenth-century English tools which closely resemble those in use in the Netherlands. The embossed floral papers made in eighteenth-century Germany were sent to the Netherlands and re-exported, and due to this became known as 'Dutch gilt'.

Trends originating in one country affected others. Late fifteenth-century bindings made for the Aragonese Kings of Naples by Baldassarre Scariglia (probably a Catalan) look very Spanish. Invading armies took national tastes with them; for example, bindings produced in Milan when it was ruled by the French in Napoleonic times are virtually indistinguishable from French bindings. Binders themselves travelled and took their skills with them. Some were forced to do so by circumstance, as with the Huguenot binders of France and the Netherlands who emigrated to England in the sixteenth century; others travelled by intent, as with the eighteenth-century Spanish binder Pascual Carsi y Vidal, sent by his government to train with French and English binders. Carsi y Vidal studied in London with the German immigrant binder John Baumgarten, making the pattern of influences even more complex. The more versatile a binder was, the more money he was likely to earn. Jacob

Krause (the court binder to the Elector of Saxony, at work in Dresden 1566–85) advertised himself as being able to bind in all styles. His work resembled the French and Italian styles much admired in Germany. The binders in countries like Portugal and Mexico often emulated the styles of a culturally dominant country, in their case Spain, yet the finished product retains a provincial look.

It is unwise to make general statements about most styles of pre-fifteenth century decoration, since the bindings which remain may not be representative. Many bindings were not decorated at all, others were the structurally separate 'treasure bindings'. Fabric-covered bindings have not survived well because of their fragility. Other bindings were consciously destroyed, for example when Oliver Cromwell's troops sacked religious houses in seventeenth-century England or during the vast upheaval of the French Revolution.

One would expect developments in art to affect the decoration of bindings. However, bookbinding styles rarely kept pace with contemporary artistic trends. For example, rococo bindings first appeared in England in the 1770s, when in the wider artistic world, neo-classicism was in vogue. Binders would use their existing tools for as long as they could, not purchasing new ones until they were sure that a style was not merely a passing whim. Sometimes the owner dictated the style; Thomas Hope 'gave the binder [Staggemeier and Welcher] his plan.... of book embellishment' for a binding tooled with antique ornaments (*see* fig. 54) on a book to be presented to the Royal Institution in London in 1805.[49]

54. Lyre motif (actual size) gold-tooled on the binding of Horace, [Works], Paris, 1799 bound by Staggemeier & Welcher. BL C.180.cc.4.

Styles can also surprise, being seemingly out of step with the 'spirit of the age'. This occurs in seventeenth-century England with the unexpectedly cheerful onlaid bindings which appeared during the Protectorate of the 1650s when the Puritans held sway.

The self-conscious notion that the decoration on a binding should reflect the contents of the text began to develop during the eighteenth century, although Bibles and prayer books often did display religious scenes, tooled with 'IHS' or pious injunctions. Devotional works were frequently given as marriage or engagement gifts, the bindings of which often featured appropriate motifs – for example,

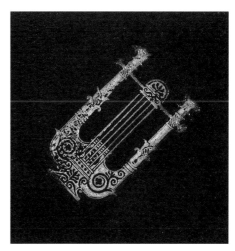

clasped hands. The figure of Fortune (common on Italian fifteenth- and sixteenth-century bindings, *see* fig. 55) would also have been suitable for bindings intended as presents.

Selected decorative styles by century

Space does not permit a comprehensive account – the following notes are confined to the recording of broad trends.

55. Fortune motif gold-tooled on Cyprian, *Opera*, Lyons, 1535. BL C.108.c.8.

56. A Coptic binding on Four Gospels [in Coptic], MS, eighth century. Photograph courtesy of the Pierpont Morgan Library (MS 569).

Fifth to Ninth centuries: Bindings featured abstract designs including interlace, gilded leather, simple punched patterns, hatched lines and sections of leather incised and cut away. Coptic bindings (*see* fig. 56) are decorated in this manner.

Tenth to Eleventh centuries: The few surviving examples are plain (not decorated) or jewelled and silver gilt treasure bindings. Textiles were used as covering materials (and also continued into the twelfth century).

Twelfth century: 'The most attractive group of blind-stamped bindings ever produced, the Romanesque bindings of the twelfth and thirteenth centuries with their delightful representations of fabulous monsters, saints and prophets'[50] were produced chiefly in Paris (*see* fig. 57), but also in Germany and England. Characteristically, the upper and lower covers feature different designs.

57. Lower cover of Paris romanesque binding on Gospels of St Matthew and St Mark. MS, [Paris, *c.*1200]. BL Davis 386.

Thirteenth century: The first panel stamp was recorded in the Netherlands. 'Tavolette', that is, painted wooden covers, began to be used to protect treasury records in Siena (*see* fig. 48). Limoges produced enamelled plaques which were nailed on to book covers of 'treasure bindings' (*see* fig. 44).

Fourteenth century: In the late fourteenth and fifteenth centuries, cut leather work appeared in the German-speaking world (*see* fig. 43) and to a lesser extent, in France, Italy, Scandinavia, the Netherlands and England. Notable practitioners of cut leather work were Mair Jaffe and Ulrich Schreier (both fifteenth century).

Fifteenth century: Early fifteenth-century designs, featuring vertical columns of repeated individual blind tooled motifs, appeared in France. German bindings were decorated with animals, rosettes, religious subjects and metalwork. Identified binders include Ulrich Frenckel, Johannes Richenbach and Joannes Fogel.

Mudéjar bindings (fifteenth- to sixteenth-century) (*see* fig. 58) made by Spanish Moors featured rope and knot work, also common in Italy (*see* fig. 59), and punches. Gold tooling was first practised in Italy, Spain (with national emblems such as lions and shells) and Hungary (on the books of King Matthias Covinus, 1458–90). Baldassarre Scariglia is known to have produced early gold-tooled bindings for the Aragonese Kings of Naples.

Late fifteenth-century panel stamps and rolls (blind-tooled) appeared in England, France and Germany, but use became more frequent in the sixteenth century. Binders included Ludovicus Ravescot in Louvain, and in England, the stationers John Reynes and

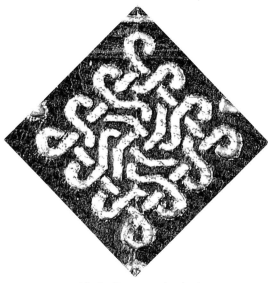

58. (LEFT) Mudéjar binding on Breviary for the use of Toledo. MS, [Toledo, late fifteenth century.]
BL Davis 656.

59. (ABOVE) Knot motif gold-tooled on the binding of *Missale Romanum*, Venice, 1506.
BL C.108.a.11.

60. (RIGHT) An 'Apollo & Pegasus' binding on Galeazzo Capella, *Commentarii*, Venice, 1539 by Maestro Luigi for GB Grimaldi.
BL Davis 766.

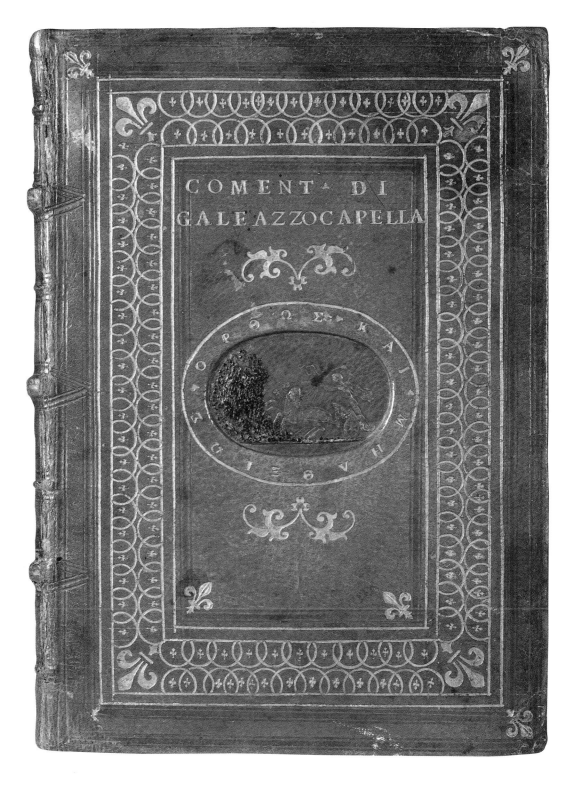

61. Vase motif gold-tooled on the binding of Seneca, *Naturalium Quaestionum libri VII*, Venice, 1522. BL Davis 780.

Martin Dature owned signed panels and rolls which were used by the (as yet unidentified) binders who worked for them.

Sixteenth century: Early sixteenth-century Italian designs were imitated because of the binders' early expertise in gold-tooling. Decorative schemes included simple painted or plain geometric interlacing ribbons, cameos (a famous example being the Apollo and Pegasus cameo appearing on bindings owned by the banker Giovanni Battista Grimaldi *see* fig. 60), mottos, Fortune holding a sail (*see* fig. 55),

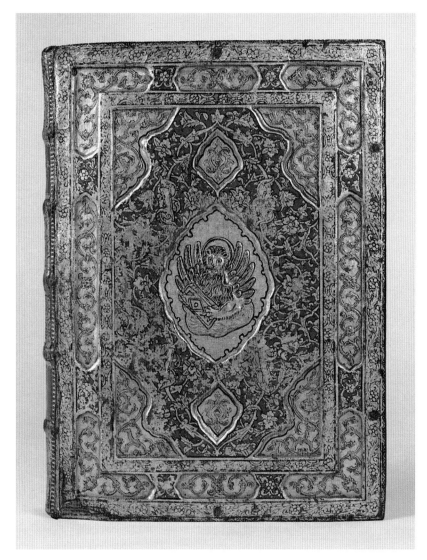

62. A painted and glazed ducale binding on *Original Commission and Instructions of Pasquale Ciconia, Doge of Venice, to Vincent Dandolo, on his appointment as consul at Alexandria*, MS., 1587. Note the sunken panels and the traces of fabric ties. BL Add. MS16996.

63. Flower motifs (actual size) gold-tooled on Lactantius, *Divinarum institutionum... libri VII*, [Lyons], 1587 bound for Pietro Duodo. BL C.69.bb.18

64. (LEFT) Pausanias, *Veteris Graeciae descriptio*, Florence, 1551 (probably bound by Picques) for Mahieu; BL Davis 403.
(RIGHT) Zacharia Ferreri, *Hymni novi ecclesiastici*, Rome, 1525 bound by Claude Picques for Jean Grolier. BL Davis 374.

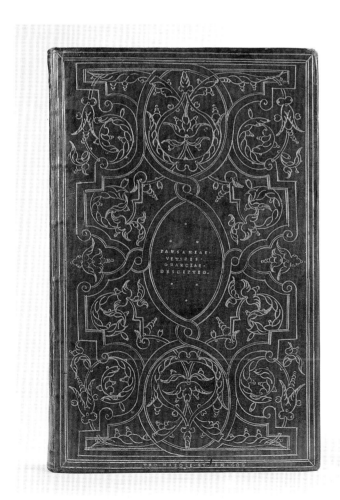

flaming urns or vases (*see* fig. 61), and rolls incorporating dolphins. An eastern influence was discernible particularly in Venetian work (*see* fig. 62).

Gold tooling was practised in France around 1507, in England around 1519 and in Germany and the Netherlands by the middle of the century. French designs included Italian-style interlacing ribbons (often called strapwork, *see* fig. 64), fleurons, arabesques, hatched tools, 'macabre' bindings (silver-tooled with mementi mori often associated with Henry III), 'semis', architectural styles, and the ebullient 'fanfare' style, also popular in the seventeenth century.

Notable figures in France include Geoffroy Tory (died 1533), the printer, publisher and engraver who designed panels; and the

65. Binding for charter issued by Philip II of Spain, *Sentencia a carta executoria de hidalguia a pedimiento de Gutierre Uruena, Vezino de la villa de Trigueros*, Valladolid, September 22, 1572. Note the fan design, the ties and the seal.
Photograph courtesy of the Hispanic Society of America.

binders Etienne Roffet, Claude Picques and Nicolas and Clovis Eve.

A style which featured small oval wreaths and flowers made for Pietro Duodo, the Venetian ambassador, was also influential (*see* fig. 63). The collections of Jean Grolier (1479–1565), Treasurer of France, and Thomas Mahieu, Secretary to Cathérine de Medicis, contained examples from the best French workshops, inscribed with the owner's name and motto (*see* fig. 64). The words 'et amicorum' were used to signify that the books were also meant for the enjoyment of the owner's friends. Thomas Wotton, a Protestant Englishman, commissioned works from Paris workshops, similarly inscribed. Jacques Auguste de Thou, President of the Parlement de Paris, had a large collection of French fanfare and armorial bindings.

English blind-tooled panels and rolls show a Netherlandish influence. Later gold-tooled work followed French patterns, for example the 'semis' and later, fanfare bindings. Heavier-looking corner and centrepiece blocks were also popular. Devotional works were frequently bound in embroidered cloth, a practice which continued until around 1660. Notable English binders include the King Edward and Queen Mary binder and Jean de Planche.

In Spain, 'Cartas de executoris de hidalguia'(patents of nobility, sixteenth- to seventeenth-century) were given ornate gold-tooled bindings with seals, cords and ribbon ties (*see* fig. 65). Gold-tooled fan motifs appeared and continued to be used.

1560–1600 has been described by H.M. Nixon as 'The Golden Age of German bookbinding'. Gold tooling was introduced into Germany by Jacob Krause, and continued by his successor Caspar Meuser. Blind-tooled bindings were also popular and remained so into the seventeenth century (*see* fig. 66). Ownership initials and dates were frequently tooled onto the covers (*see* fig. 41).

Blind-tooled styles continued to be favoured in the Netherlands, and Jan Ryckaert produced examples in Ghent. There was no early tradition of tooling in gold, but by the 1540s, sophisticated gold-tooled work was being produced, mostly in the French style. This is the case with the Antwerp bindery associated with the printer Christophe Plantin, who trained as a binder in Paris but was forced to give up working at the bench himself due to an accident. Gold-tooled oval centrepieces and large corner blocks were also fashionable.

Pierced leather and vellum bindings appeared in the sixteenth and seventeenth centuries, especially on the continent, but were rare.

66. 'Heads in medallions' roll featuring Protestant reformers blind-tooled on the binding of Leonhard Fronsperger, *Bauw Ordnung. Von Burger und Nachbarlichen Gebeuwen*, Frankfurt, 1564. BL C.66.h.11.

67. (ABOVE) Seventeenth-century French fanfare binding on *Adnotationes et Meditationes in Euangelia*, Antwerp, 1596 by Macé Ruette.
BL C.183.b.3.

68. (ABOVE RIGHT) *Concilia Limana*, Rome, 1684, bound in a gold-tooled Italian armorial binding featuring a characteristic floral roll, fish scale tooling, and basketwork. The type of hat reflects the owner's status in society or, in this case, the church.
BL C.66.g.8.

Seventeenth century: France remained influential and from the 1630s, pointillé tools (*see* fig. 35) were developed there and spread to England and the Netherlands. Notable binders included Macé Ruette (*see* fig. 67), and Florimond Badier. French fan/wheel and fanfare designs were imitated in Italy (as in fig. 68) and contined to appear in Spain. Colourful mosaic bindings emerged, to become more popular in the eighteenth century. Dentelle (lace work borders) and ostensibly plain Jansenist bindings (with elaborately tooled doublures) came later. In Italy, lattice-work and a fish scale pattern accompanied fan/wheel motifs. Popes and Cardinals favoured these ornate styles combined with their coats of arms (*see* fig. 68).

Mid-seventeenth-century English binders preferred colourful leather onlays, and pointillé and drawer handle tools (the latter were also common in the Netherlands (*see* fig. 69). Designs included 'sombre' (blind-tooled black leather) and 'cottage roof' styles (*see* fig. 6). The royal binders, Samuel Mearne (1624–83) and his son Charles, ran one of the most successful workshops of the day. Other binders included Robert Steel and the four 'Queens' binders' named A, B, C, and D.

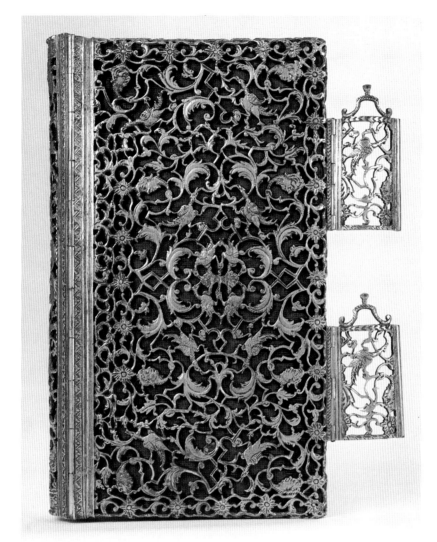

69. Drawer handle motifs (actual size) gold-tooled on the binding of *La Bible*, Amsterdam, 1678. BL C.143.a.6.

70. Eighteenth-century Swiss silver binding on *Das Neue Testament*, Zurich, 1731. BL Davis 596.

The major figure in the Netherlands was Albertus Magnus (active 1669–1689). Animals and birds in vines often appeared on rolls. Many prize bindings featuring municipal coats of arms on white vellum or treated calf were produced. Religious motifs including the Virgin and Child and 'IHS' were common, particularly in Germany. Silver bindings on devotional texts were made in Germany, Holland, Switzerland (*see* fig. 70), and Scandinavia.

Eastern European bindings on Bibles often featured corner and centrepiece designs depicting the Four Evangelists or scenes from the

71. Cornerpiece gold-tooled on the binding of
[Liturgical Epistles in Rumanian], [1812].
BL C.66.i.10.

72. Apollodorus, Bibliotheca, MS, sixteenth century,
bound by Christopher Chapman for Lord Harley.
BL Harl MS 5732.

New Testament (*see* fig. 71). These were either stamped directly on to the leather or engraved or embossed into metal plates which were then nailed to the boards.

Eighteenth century: Dentelle and mosaic styles reached the height of their popularity in France and spread to Spain and Italy. Notable binders included the Derome and Padeloup families, Augustin Duseuil and Pierre-Paul Dubuisson.

Later in the century, the French Empire style, with Greek and Egyptian motifs, followed in the wake of Napoleonic campaigns. Bradel, Tessier and the elder Bozérian were influential.

Spanish binders used rococo motifs and painted split-calf 'Pasta Espanola' bindings. Antonio da Sancha and his son Gabriel ran important workshops (*see* fig. 53b). In Italy, lattice work continued to appear and also motifs in compartments. There was a taste for highly decorated styles, especially the baroque bindings of Joseph Bona of Rome (*see* fig. 50).

In England, early in the century, the Harleian style of borders and diamond-shaped centres composed with small tools, dominated (*see* fig. 72).

The later neo-classical motifs, designed by James Stuart and Robert Adam, influenced binders in France, Germany and Spain. There was also a taste for the rococo, as practised by John Baumgarten (one of the many immigrant German binders) and Scott of Edinburgh. The most famous of the century, English binder Roger Payne (1739–97), decorated his bindings simply with small tools (*see* fig. 8).

Scottish binders used fan/wheel designs (*see* fig. 73), also a herringbone pattern. White onlays were a feature of Irish bindings.

In the Netherlands, Amsterdam and The Hague were important centres. Bindings of treated calf were popular, as were motifs with drawer handles with dots and crowns.

73. Gold-tooled fan/wheel decoration on *The Holy Bible*, Edinburgh, 1743. BL Davis 249.

In Germany, gold-tooled brown calf bindings with the stamp of Abbot Placidus Seiz (1703–36) made for Ettal Abbey in Bavaria, are particularly well known. There was a taste for 'peasant' bindings with flowers, mottos and hearts gold-tooled on coloured vellum; rococo motifs appeared later. Many books in monastic libraries were rebound in vellum or had their bindings painted white.

Nineteenth century: From the 1820s, the invention of graining plates, cheap book cloth and machines which produced book covers (independently of the texts they contained) heralded the industrialisation of the trade.

In Germany, the workshop of Johann Gerbers and family was successful. Art and literature came to be influential in binding design, the Romantic movement in particular.

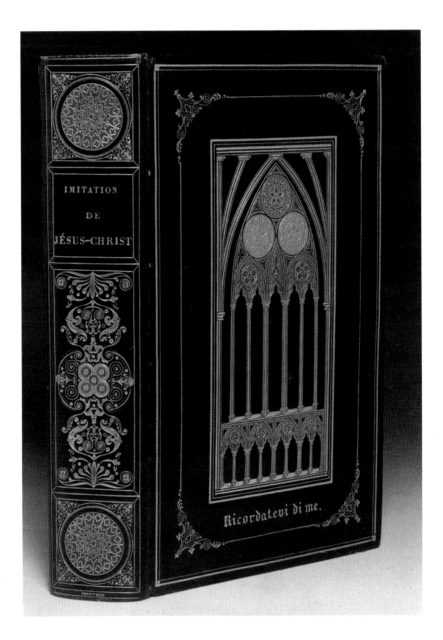

74. Cathedral binding on [Thomas à Kempis] *Imitation de Jésus-Christ*, Paris, 1823 by Joseph Thouvenin. The binder's signature has been tooled in gold at the foot of the spine.
Photograph courtesy of Sotheby's, London.

In Spain, a gold-tooled curtain design appeared, consisting of lines radiating outwards and bounded by a scalloped edge. The royal binder Antonio Suarez was influential.

There was a widespread fashion for 'historical' styles. Patrons encouraged binders to imitate bindings from the past, especially French sixteenth-century designs. The French binders Thouvenin (*see*

fig. 74), Purgold, Simier, and later Bauzonnet and the English binders Charles Lewis and Francis Bedford followed the trend. Blind- and gold-tooled 'Gothic' bindings with heavy boards and false spine bands were particularly popular in England. Cathedral bindings, made by blocking in gold, blind or colour, also evoked the past.

The Italian I F Joni took advantage of this retrospective mood by faking painted wooden book covers, imitating the Sienese 'tavolette'. In Belgium, Louis Hagué produced bindings purporting to be sixteenth-century French.

Embossed bindings were also in demand particularly in Britain and America (*see* fig. 75).

Towards the end of the century, a reaction set in and binders followed new artistic trends. In 1876, Jean Marius Michel and his son Henri set up a bindery in Paris which produced original designs inspired by the texts of the books being bound, and by movements like art nouveau (*see* fig. 76). Similarly, Thomas James Cobden-Sanderson (1840–1922), a follower of William Morris's Arts and Crafts movement, who first trained as a lawyer, introduced his own

75. (ABOVE LEFT) American embossed binding on Willis Clark, (ed.), *The Parlour Scrap Book*, Philadelphia, 1836 by Gaskill. BL C.129.k.15

76. (ABOVE) Doublure of Jeanne Julia Regnault, *Causerie sur l'art dramatique*, Paris 1903 bound by Marius Michel. The binder's name can be seen at the tail edge. BL C.108.gg.27.

81

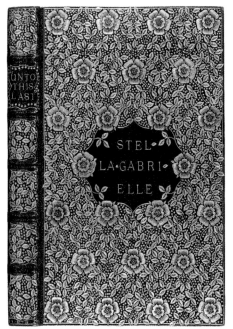

77. John Ruskin, *Unto This Last*, 1884 bound by T.J Cobden-Sanderson for his daughter, Stella. BL C.68.h.17.

style based on dazzling gold-tooling (*see* fig. 77). His Doves Bindery in Hammersmith (1893) influenced the next generation of binders. This revival in the craft was bolstered by the formation of the Guild of Women Binders and its male counterpart, the Hampstead Bindery, and the provision of binding classes in art schools.

The foremost American binder, William Matthews, was in fact a Scot. He encouraged the members of the Grolier Club to promote fine bindings and presided over the formation of the club's bindery in 1895.

Twentieth century: The early part of the century has been dominated by French and English work, although certain names do stand out from other countries, such as Paul Kerston who bound and taught in Berlin. The new wave was continued by French binders such as Pierre Legrain (1888–1929) who incorporated typography into binding design, a practice continued by Pierre-Lucian Martin. The Belgian-born designer Paul Bonet (1889–1971) (*see* fig. 78) was influenced by Cubism and Surrealism. The Société de la Reliure Originale (founded in Paris in 1946) still works to ensure that

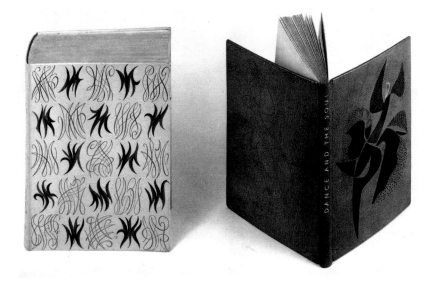

78. (LEFT) André Malraux, *Romans*, Paris, 1951 designed by Paul Bonet. BL C.109.c.18.
(RIGHT) Paul Valèry, *Dance and the soul*, London, 1951 bound by Edgar Mansfield. BL C.130.c.6.

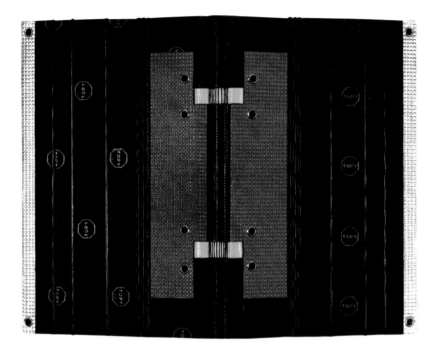

79. Jean Epstein, *Cinéma*, Paris, 1921 bound by Jean de Gonet in 1985, incorporating aluminium strips and black plasticised rubber (the type used on the soles of shoes). BL C.188.a.19

new developments continue. In the United Kingdom, binderies associated with private presses flourished in the 1920s and 1930s, such as the Gregynog Press bindery run by George Fisher. The Designer Bookbinders (initially founded in 1951 but reorganised under this name in 1968) continue to be influential. One of its founders, Edgar Mansfield, is considered to be the father of modern binding design in England (*see* fig. 78).

Other notable binders include J.A. Szirmai working in the Netherlands, Kurt Lodenburg, Ignatz Wiemeler, and Otto Dorfner in Germany, Gustaf Hedberg in Sweden, Jeff Clements, C. Philip Smith and Sally Lou Smith in Britain, Micheline de Bellefroid and Jean de Gonet in France, and the Spanish Emilio Brugalla. Modern materials have inspired binders to incorporate unusual surfaces into their designs, for example the aluminium and plasticised rubber used by Jean de Gonet (*see* fig. 79). Bindings, influenced by contemporary movements in art, have subsequently become works of art in themselves.

The Management of Bindings Collections

Compiling records

Only a visual record will serve to identify an individual binding. Tools can be so similar that a written description is ineffective and misleading. A photocopy of the binding provides a cheap and effective record of it and does not cause damage. This process can even produce an adequate reproduction of blind-tooled bindings.

An alternative is to make rubbings of tooling (*see* fig. 80) with a fairly soft pencil and thin paper (the technique is similar to rubbing brasses). This is best left to someone experienced, since delicate or fragile leather can be easily damaged and gold or paint can be lifted onto the underside of the paper if too much pressure is used. It is helpful to protect the rubbing by spraying it with an aerosol fixative available from art shops.

80. Pencil rubbing of blind-tooled motif from an English fifteenth-century imitation of a romanesque binding. BL IA 55454.

The benefit of both photocopies and rubbings is that they reproduce actual-size images of the tooling, which is not the case in many catalogues where illustrations are frequently enlarged or reduced.

A brief written description is also useful. There is no universally accepted standard terminology for describing a binding, although there are works which help (*see* Further Reading). It is a good idea to look at existing catalogues for guidance as to the format of description.

Bindings can now be scanned, digitised and stored in computer databases. This allows

for minute examination of the binding, but it is important to remember that there must be a facility for establishing a life-size reproduction of the tooling.

Storage and exhibitions

A steady temperature of between 16°C to 18°C and a constant relative humidity within the range 45% to 55% is recommended. Vellum is more delicate and should ideally be stored in a colder, dryer atmosphere. Boxing vellum bindings will protect the covers from warping. Conditions should be constant; fluctuation is more dangerous than storage at consistent, if not ideal, levels of temperature and humidity.

Bindings should be protected from daylight. If daylight is unavoidable, windows should be curtained or fitted with filters to prevent damage by ultra-violet light which will quickly fade bindings.

Environmental considerations are similar to those required for storage, but attention should be paid to lighting levels, which ought not to exceed 50 lux. Tungsten bulbs are recommended as they do not generate heat. Conditions should not vary too much from storage area to exhibition case.

Books must be treated as individual items, taking different sizes and structures into account. This is especially relevant with modern bindings, many of which do not conform to traditional book formats. L-shapes, wedges and cradles (necessary if the book is to be shown open) made to archival standard are commercially available, but sound structures can be improvised with the imaginative use of whatever is at hand, providing the materials are acid-free (or covered with acid-free paper).

The most effective way of displaying a binding is at a gentle slope with proper support for the whole of the closed book; a perspex L-shape either free-standing or screwed into a sloping back board is a simple method. A perspex fillet cut to the size of the text block should be used to prevent it pulling away from the covers. Heavy and/or large books must lie flat. If the inside of the binding is to be shown, for example to display decorated end-leaves or doublures, wedge-shapes or cradles should support the opened cover.

The British Standard document[51] (currently being revised) gives useful guidelines for optimum storage and exhibition conditions.

Notes

1 *See*, for example, M.M. Foot, *The History of Bookbinding as a Mirror of Society*' (London, 1998).

2 'Gilt edges' in *The Bookbinder*, vol 1, 1888, p.67.

3 H.M. Nixon & M.M. Foot, *A History of English Decorated Bookbindings* (Oxford, 1992), p.92 (cited below as 'Nixon & Foot, *History*').

4 H.M. Nixon 'Harleian bindings' in *Studies in the Book Trade in Honour of Graham Pollard* (Oxford, 1975), p.171 (cited below as Nixon, 'Harleian bindings').

5 M.M. Foot, *Studies in the History of Bookbinding* (Aldershot, 1993), p.2 (cited below as Foot, *Studies*). A description of manuals is given in Graham Pollard and Esther Potter's *Early Bookbinding Manuals* (Oxford, 1984).

6 H M Nixon, *Catalogue of the Pepys Library at Magdalene College Cambridge*, vol VI: Bindings, (Woodbridge, 1984), p.xiii (cited below as Nixon, *Catalogue of the Pepys Library*).

7 'Detached thoughts on books and reading' in *Essays on Elia or The Superannuated Man* (London, 1927), p.13.

8 Dudley Carleton quoted in R. Birley, 'The history of Eton College Library', *The Library*, 5th ser., II (1956), p.248.

9 An anonymous author of *A General Description of all Trades* (1747) quoted by Bernard C. Middleton in *A History of English Craft Bookbinding Technique* (London, 1996), p.258.

10 Ellic Howe, *A List of London Bookbinders 1648-1815* (London, 1950), p.xvi.

11 John Jaffray, *A collection of manuscripts relating to the art and trade of bookbinding*, vol IV, London, 1864 (Ms.) p.2. A typescript of this volume is in the British Library and further references refer to the page numbers of the type-written version.

12 John Dunton, *Life and Errors* (London, 1705), p.340.

13 H.M. Nixon *Broxbourne Library: Styles and Designs of Bookbindings from the Twelfth to the Twentieth Century* (London, 1956), p.244 (cited below as 'Nixon, *Broxbourne*').

14 John Dunton, *op. cit.*, p.341.

15 Compiled by Philippa Bernard with Leo Bernard & Angus O'Neill, *Antiquarian books. A companion* (Aldershot, 1994), p.323.

16 Letter from Roger to his patron, the bookseller Thomas Payne, quoted in Foot, *Studies*, p.221.

17 H.M. Nixon, *English Restoration Bookbinding* (London, 1974), p.16.

18 H.M. Nixon, *Sixteenth-century Gold-tooled Bookbindings in the Pierpont Morgan Library* (New York, 1971), p. 217 (cited below as 'Nixon, *Pierpont Morgan*').

19 M.M. Foot, *The Henry Davis Gift* (London, 1978), I, p.287.

20 John Jaffray, *op. cit.*, p.19.

21 John Jaffray, *op. cit.*, p.4.

22 T.F. Dibdin, *The Bibliographical Decameron* (London, 1817), II, p.522.

23 Dibdin, *op. cit.*, p.511.

24 Quoted in H.M. Nixon, *Twelve Books in Fine Bindings from the Library of J.W. Hely-Hutchinson* (London, 1953), p.71.

25 Nixon, *Broxbourne*, p.244. See fig. 107 of Bernard C. Middleton, *op. cit*, for an illustration of a binding executed by Price.

26 Jaffray, *op. cit.*, p.184.

27 Marianne Tidcombe, *Women Bookbinders 1880-1920* (London, 1996), p.24.

28 The letter is quoted in T.W. Hanson, 'Edwards of Halifax bookbinders' in *Book Handbook*, VI, 1948, p.337.

29 *Instructions for the Erecting of a Library*, 1661.

30 R. Latham & W. Matthews, (eds.) *The Diary of Samuel Pepys* (London, 1976), ix, p.480.

31 Foot, *Studies*, p.432.

32 Lisa Jardine, *Worldly Goods* (London, 1996), p.140.

33 Nixon, *Pierpont Morgan*, p.120.

34 Maurice Picquard, 'Les livres du Cardinal de Granvelle à la Bibliothèque de Besançon', *Libri* , 1, 1951, 308-9.

35 Geoffrey Keynes 'John Evelyn as bibliophile', *The Library*, 4th series, vol.xii, 1932, 188.

36 B.L. Lansdowne MS 17 (f.63).

37 John Jaffray, *op. cit.*, p.188.

38 Quoted in Foot, *Studies*, p.318.

39 Lady Holland, *A Memoir* (London, 1885), p.32.

40 Nixon, *Catalogue of the Pepys Library*, p.xvi.

41 BL MS Cotton Domitian A. VII, ff. 1, 84v.

42 T. Fuller, *The History of the Worthies of England* (London, 1662), ii, p.48.

43 Joseph McDonnell & Patrick Healy, *Gold-tooled bookbindings commissioned by Trinity College Dublin in the eighteenth century* (Dublin, 1987), p.xiv.

44 Bernard C. Middleton, *op. cit.*, p.34.

45 H.E. Bates, *The World in Ripeness* (London, 1972), p.89.

46 Douglas Leighton, *Modern Bookbinding* (London, 1935), p.26.

47 P. Hentzner, *Itinerarium Germaniae, Galliae; Angliae; Italiae* (Nuremberg, 1612), translated by Richard Bentley, *A Journey into England in the Year 1598* and published at Strawberry Hill by Horace Walpole in 1757, p.31.

48 Charles Southey (ed.), *The Life and Correspondence of the Late Robert Southey* (London, 1850), vol. vi., p.17.

49 Dibdin, *op. cit.*, p.205.

50 H.M. Nixon quoted in P.H. Muir (ed.), *Talks on Book Collecting* (London, 1952) p.62.

51 BS 5454:1989 British Standard Recommendations for Storage and exhibition of archival documents, British Standards Institution, 1989.

Glossary

* indicates term included on diagram of binding structure, fig. 17 on page 30.

alum — a salt used to prepare a skin for binding, rendering it soft, flexible, and white in colour (see tawing).

azured — an heraldic term used to describe a pattern comprising closely spaced parallel, diagonal lines (sometimes called 'hatched'), see fig. 36.

bands * — ridges, visible on the spine, which accommodate cords (or other sewingsupports) on which the text block is sewn.

blind-tooling (or blind-stamping) — a method of decoration whereby a heated binding tool makes a plain impression in the leather or cloth (gold leaf or colours are not used).

bolts — the folds at the head, tail or fore-edge of a folded sheet which must be cut before the pages can be turned. The fold at the spine edge is sewn through.

caoutchouc — binding in which loose leaves are glued (not sewn) together to form the text block by means of a rubber solution: a nineteenth-century invention (sometimes called 'gutta percha').

case — boards, spine and cover made separately from text block (often associated with edition bindings).

chemise — a protective covering of fabric or soft leather which wraps over the entire binding.

codex (pl. codices) — structure comprising covers and writing material fastened at one side to open like a book, as opposed to scrolls.

dentelle — an outer border on the inside or outside of a cover comprising small tooled motifs, resembling lace.

doreur — French term for a craftsman who specialises in gold-tooling.

doublure * — ornamental lining in leather or cloth used in place of a pasted down end-leaf.

Dutch gilt — a style of decorated paper (imported into the Netherlands from Germany) commonly featuring embossed gold flowers on a multi-coloured background, see fig. 23.

endbands — collective name to describe headbands and tailbands.

end-leaves — papers (decorated or plain) pasted or sewn in to protect the text block from the covers. Comprises the paste-down (pasted to the inside cover) and the fly-leaf, or free end-leaf , which lies next to the text block.

fanfare — a style of binding featuring leafy sprays and interlaces bounded by a single gold line on one side and a double gold line on the other, see fig. 67.

fillet — a continuous plain line produced by a wheel-shaped finishing tool of the same name.

finishing — a technical term for decorating the binding, particularly gold-tooling.

fly-leaf * — the end-leaf which is not pasted down to the inner cover (sometimes called the free end-leaf).

fore-edge * — the edge of the text block opposite the spine.

forwarding — the process of making the structure of a binding.

full binding — a single material covers the entire binding, e.g. full leather or full buckram, see fig. 6.

furniture — anything attached to the boards, e.g.

clasps, metal cornerpieces or bosses.

gauffering   the decoration of the gilded edge of a text block with impressed designs, *see* fig. 28.

girdle book   a book with covering material extended at the top to enable it to be hooked to a belt.

gold-tooling   a method of decoration involving the impressing of heated tools through gold leaf, into the leather or cloth.

Greek style   used (particularly in the fifteenth and sixteenth centuries) on the bindings of classical Greek texts, characterised by the extension of the spine leather at head and tail to protect double endbands, also, grooved wooden boards, and four clasps of plaited leather catching onto pins, *see* fig. 24.

gutta-percha   *see* caoutchouc.

half binding   one material covers the the spine and corners (e.g. vellum) and a different material covers the boards (eg decorated paper).

hatched   *see* azured and fig. 36.

headband   small core (e.g. leather or vellum) wrapped with threads, which projects slightly beyond the top of text block spine. It is protective and decorative.

hollow back   a binding in which the covering material is not affixed directly to the back of the sewn sections but to a paper liner, often called a 'tube'.

journeyman   a trained craftsman who did not own his own business but hired out his skills.

kettle stitch   made near the head and tail of each section of a book to link it to the preceeding one (sometimes called a 'catch stitch').

limp   describes a binding without stiffened boards.

marbling   the process of producing marble-like patterns. When applied to leather, the pattern is created by the application of acid or inks; when applied to paper or fore-edges, it is achieved with pigment.

morocco   a type of goatskin which originated in Morocco.

Mudéjar   binding decorated with intricate Islamic style designs featuring interlaces, knots and punch work, *see* fig. 58. Initially practised by Christianised Moors (Mudéjars) in fifteenth-century Spain.

pallet   finishing tool which produces lines or long, narrow decorative strips used on spines. A name pallet impresses the binder's name on a signed binding.

parchment   sheep or goatskin (with the hair removed) which has been split, soaked, limed, and dried under tension, not tanned like leather.

paring   the process of thinning leather.

paste-down *   the end-leaf which is pasted to the inside of the boards.

perfect   binding in which the loose leaves of a text block are glued together, not sewn. A modern version of the caoutchouc binding. Many paperbacks are perfect bound.

pointillé   term used to describe motif outlined with dots, *see* fig. 35.

publisher's binding   binding, (often cloth), commissioned by a publisher in which the text block is made independently from its enclosing cloth case. A whole edition would be produced in this format.

quarter binding   one material covers the spine (e.g. vellum) and a different material (e.g. decorated paper) covers the boards.

reliure   a French term for a binding.

roan   a type of sheepskin.

russia   tanned hide treated with birch-bark oil, frequently diced (incised with intersecting diagonal lines).

semi-limp   binding with boards of thin, flexible card.

semis (semé)   an heraldic term used to describe a background of scattered small tooled motifs, *see* fig.12.

sewing support   thongs or cords placed horizontally across sections of leaves and incorporated into the sewing. These often form the basis for the bands visible on the outside of the spine.

signatures   small letters and numbers printed at the beginning of each quire or section to enable these to be bound in order.

signed binding   one in which the craftsman's name is displayed either by tooling in gold or blind, ink stamping on the end-leaves, or pasting in a printed trade label.

slips   strips of thin vellum used as sewing supports. Often visible on the front covers of vellum bindings.

sombre   a style of binding (frequently used on

devotional works) featuring blind tooling on black leather.

square * a technical term for the inside edge of the boards of a binding which projects beyond the text block, usually measured to the thickness of the board. Often covered by the turn-in.

stabbing a method of sewing where thread is passed through the sides of folded sheets rather than taken through each fold; so called after the holes stabbed to accommodate the thread.

stamps / tools engraved or cast dies which impress decorative motifs. Traditionally the term 'stamp' has been used when describing early (e.g. fifteenth- and sixteenth-century) bindings, and 'tool' refers to the later period.

standing press a large, heavy, floor-standing press, capable of exerting great pressure.

stationery binding used for binding blank books intended to be written in e.g. ledgers and account books. Frequently bound in vellum.

tailband small core (of leather, vellum etc.) wrapped with threads, which projects slightly beyond the tail of text block spine It is protective and decorative.

tanning the preparation of a skin which turns it into leather. Immersion in tanning liquid made from vegetable materials renders it durable (see also tawing).

tawing the preparation of a skin (usually pig or goat) by treating it with a mixture based on aluminium salts, which renders it flexible. An early alternative to tanning.

text block * the sections which make up the text of the book.

tight back a binding in which the covering material is affixed directly to the backs of the sections, i.e. there is no 'hollow'.

tipping in the process of inserting a sheet or section by applying a thin line of paste to a single edge.

trade binding pre-nineteenth-century books which were not bound up to the taste of the purchaser, but bound before sale, as with nineteenth-century publishers' bindings.

treasure binding cases, often made of precious or jewelled metal, which were not an integral part of the binding, but could be passed from text to text (the text blocks were slipped inside).

tree calf calfskin treated with acid to form a
(tree marble) design on the covers, which resembles the branches of a tree.

turkey type of goatskin, later known as morocco, see fig. 6.

turn in * the edge of the covering material (usually leather or cloth) folded over and pasted to the inside boards of a binding.

vellum calfskin, which has been soaked, limed (with the hair removed) and dried under tension, not tanned like leather, see fig. 51.

wrappers the covers of a binding which has no boards. They can be paper or vellum, see fig. 23 for binding with plain blue paper wrappers.

Further Reading

Bibliographies

F.A. Schmidt-Künsemüller, *Bibliographie zur Geschichte der Einbandkunst*, Wiesbaden, 1987. [The coverage is wide and not confined to the German-speaking world. It is easy for the non-German speaker to use and includes useful indexes referring to binders and authors of works on the history of bookbinding.]

R. Myers, *The British Book Trade, from Caxton to the present day*, London, 1973, pp. 25–40.

Annual Bibliography of the History of the Printed Book and Libraries, The Hague, 1973–

Bibliographie der Buch- und Bibliotheksgeschichte, Bad Iburg, 1982–

General works, Histories, General collections
(Many of the following also contain useful bibliographies.)

American Library Association, *Binding Terms*, Chicago, 1988.

Bodleian Library, *Fine bindings 1500–1700 from Oxford Libraries*. Catalogue of an Exhibition, Oxford, 1968.

J. Carter, *ABC for Book Collectors*, London, 1980.

P. Gaskell, *A New Introduction to Bibliography*, Oxford, 1985, pp.146–159, 231–250.

W.Y. Fletcher, *Bookbinding in England and France*, London, 1897.

M.M. Foot, *The Henry Davis Gift*, 2 vols., London, 1978–1983.

M.M. Foot, *Pictorial bookbindings*, London, 1986.

M.M. Foot, *Studies in the History of Bookbinding*, London, 1993.

M.M. Foot, *The History of Bookbinding as a Mirror of Society*, London, 1998.

E.P. Goldschmidt, *Gothic and Renaissance Bookbindings*, London, 1928, reprinted Amsterdam, 1967.

J.P. Harthan, *Bookbindings*, London, 1984.

H. Hedvig, *Handbuch der Einbandkunde*, 3 vols, Hamburg, 1953–55.

G.D. Hobson, *Bindings in Cambridge Libraries*, Cambridge, 1929.

G.D. Hobson, 'Some Early Bindings and Binders' tools' in *The Library*, 4th series, 19, 1938–9, pp. 202–249.

O. Mazal, *Europäische Einbandkunst aus Mittelalter und Neuzeit*, Graz, 1990.

D. Miner, *The History of Bookbinding 525–1950*, Baltimore, 1957.

National Preservation Office (British Library), *Glossary*, London, 1992.

P. Needham, *Twelve Centuries of Bookbindings 400–1600*, New York & London, 1979.

H.M. Nixon, *Broxbourne Library; Styles and Designs of Bookbindings from the twelfth to the twentieth century*, London, 1956.

H.M. Nixon, *Sixteenth-century Gold-tooled Bookbindings in the Pierpont Morgan Library*, New York, 1971.

J.B. Oldham, *Shrewsbury School Library Bindings*, Oxford, 1943.

G. Pollard, 'Describing Medieval bookbindings' in *Medieval Learning and Literature: Essays presented to Richard William Hunt*, Oxford, 1976, pp. 50–65.

M.T. Roberts & D. Etherington, *Bookbinding and the Conservation of Books. A Dictionary of Descriptive Terminology*, Washington, 1982. This is also available on the Internet.

M. Tidcombe, *Women Bookbinders 1880–1920*, London, 1996.

W.H.J. Weale, *Bookbindings and Rubbings of Bindings in the National Art Library, South Kensington Museum*, 2 vols., London, 1898–1894.

W.H.J. Weale, *Early Stamped Bookbindings in the British Museum... completed by Lawrence Taylor*, London, 1922.

H. Wheatley, *Remarkable bindings in the British Museum*, London, 1889.

Sales catalogues from Christie Manson & Woods Ltd, Bernard Quaritch Ltd, Maggs Bros. Ltd, Sotheby & Co.

British bindings

D. Ball, *Victorian publishers' bindings*, London, 1985.

J. Carter, *Publisher's cloth; an outline history of publisher's binding in England, 1820–1900*, New York, 1935.

M. Craig, *Irish Bookbindings 1600–1800*, London, 1954.

Designer Bookbinders, 'British Bookbinding in the Twentieth Century', vol. 14 of *The New Bookbinder*, 1994.

W.Y. Fletcher, *English Bookbindings in the British Museum*, London, 1895.

G.D. Hobson, *English Bindings before 1500*, Cambridge, 1929.

G.D. Hobson, *English Bindings 1490–1940 in the Library of J R Abbey*, London, 1940.

E. Howe, *A List of London Bookbinders, 1648–1815*, London, 1950.

E. Jamieson, *English Embossed Bindings 1825–1850*, Cambridge, 1972.

J. McDonnell, *Five Hundred Years of the Art of the Book in Ireland*, Dublin, 1997.

R. McLean, *Victorian Publisher's Bookbindings in cloth and leather*, London, 1930.

W.S. Mitchell, *A History of Scottish Bookbinding 1432 to 1650*, Edinburgh, 1955.

H.M. Nixon, *English Restoration Bookbinding. Samuel Mearne and his contemporaries*, London, 1974.

H.M. Nixon, *Five Centuries of English Bookbinding*, London, 1978.

H.M. Nixon & M.M. Foot, *A History of Decorated Bookbinding in England*, Oxford, 1992.

J.B. Oldham, *English Blind-stamped Bindings*, Cambridge, 1952.

J.B. Oldham, *Blind Panels of English Binders*, Cambridge, 1958.

M. Packer, *Bookbinders of Victorian England*, London, 1991.

G. Pollard, 'The Names of some English fifteenth-century binders', in *The Library*, 5th series, XXV, 1970, pp. 193–218.

C. Ramsden, *Bookbinders of the United Kingdom (outside London) 1780–1840*, London, 1954, reprinted 1987.

C. Ramsden, *London bookbinders 1790–1840*, London, 1956.

M. Sadleir, *The evolution of publishers' binding styles 1770–1900*, London, 1930.

M.J. Somerland, *Scottish 'Wheel' and 'Herringbone' bindings in the Bodleian Library*, Oxford, 1967.

Continental bindings

Bibliotheca Wittockiana, *Ocho siglos de Encuadernacion Española*, Brussels, 1985.

Bibliotheca Wittockiana, *Quatre siècles de reliure en Belgique 1500–1900*, Brussels, 1993.

British Museum, *Bindings from the library of Jean Grolier*, London, 1965 [by H.M. Nixon].

T. De Marinis, *La Legatura artistica in Italia nel secoli XV e XVI*, Florence, 1960.

R. Devauchelle, *La reliure en France*, 3 vols., Paris, 1959–61.

Y. Deveux, *Dix siècles de reliure*, Paris, 1977.

A. Duncan & G. de Bartha, *Art Nouveau and Art Deco Bookbinding: The French Masterpieces, 1880–1940*, Paris, 1989.

S. Fogelmark, *Flemish and Related Panel-stamped bindings*, New York, 1990.

D. Gid, *Catalogue des reliures françaises estampée à froid XVe–XVIe siècle de la Bibliothèque Mazarine*, 2 vols., Paris, 1984.

L. Gruel, *Manuel historique et bibliographique de l'amateur de reliures*, 2 vols., Paris, 1887–1905.

A.R.A. Hobson, *Apollo and Pegasus. An enquiry into the formation and disposal of a Renaissance library*, Amsterdam, 1975.

A.R.A. Hobson, *French and Italian Collectors and their Bindings illustrated from Examples in the Library of J R Abbey*, Oxford, 1953.

A.R.A. Hobson, *Humanists and Bookbinders*, Cambridge, 1989.

G.D. Hobson, *Les reliures à la fanfare*, Amsterdam, 1970.

K. Haebler, *Rollen- und Plattenstempel des XVI. Jahrhunderts*, (Sammlung Bibliothekswissenschaftlicher Arbeiten, Heft 41–2), Leipzig, 1928–1929.

Hispanic Society of America, *An album of selected bookbindings*, New York, 1967 [by C L Penney]

E. Kyriss, *Verzierte gotische Einbände im altern deutschen Sprachgebiet*, Stuttgart, 1951.

L-M. Michon, *La Reliure Française*, Paris, 1951.

L-M. Michon, *Les Reliures Mosaiquées du XVIIIe Siècle*, Paris, 1956.

C. Ramsden, *French bookbinders 1789–1848*, London, 1950.

M. López Serrano, *Biblioteca de Palacio Encuadernaciones*, Madrid, 1950.

H. Thomas, *Early Spanish Bookbindings, XI–XV Centuries*, London, 1939.

E. Thoinan, *Les Reliures Françaises 1500–1800*, Paris, 1893.

Islamic and Oriental

D. Haldane, *Islamic Bookbindings*, London, 1983.

B Regemorter, *Some Early Bindings from Egypt in the Chester Beatty Library*, Dublin, 1958

B. Regemorter, *Some Oriental Bindings in the Chester Beatty Library*, Dublin, 1961

United States of America

Sue Allen & Charles Gullans, *Decorated cloth in American publishers' bindings, 1840–1910*, [Los Angeles], 1994.

Bryn Mawr College Library, *Bookbinding in America 1680–1910*, Pennsylvania, 1983.

H. Lehmann-Haupt (ed.), *Bookbinding in America*, New York & London, 1967.

E. Wolfe II, *From Gothic Windows to Peacocks: American Embossed Leather*, Philadelphia, 1990.

Armorial bindings

C.J.H. Davenport, *English Heraldic Book-stamps*, London, 1909. [This is useful for the illustrations but the attributions are not always correct.]

J. Fairbairn, *Fairbairn's Book of Crests of the families of Great Britain and Ireland*, New York & London, 1993.

J. Guigard, *Nouvel armorial du Bibliophile*, 2 vols., Paris, 1890.

E. Oliver, G. Hermal & R. de Roton, *Manuel de l'amateur de reliures armoriées Françaises*, Paris, 1924–38.

Decorated papers

P. Easton, *Marbling, a history and bibliography*, Los Angeles, 1983.

A. Haemmerle, *Buntpapier*, Munich, 1961.

R.B. Loring, *Decorated Bookpapers*, Cambridge, (Ma), 1973.

R.J. Wolfe, *Marbled paper: its history, techniques and patterns*, Pennsylvania, 1990.

Embroidered bindings

G. Barber, *Textile and Embroidered Bindings*, Oxford, 1971.

C.J.H. Davenport, *English Embroidered Bookbindings*, London, 1899. [This volume is well illustrated but the text is out of date.]

Fore-edges

M.M. Foot, 'Medieval Painted Book Edges' in her *Studies of the history of bookbinding*, see above, pp. 439–454.

T.K. Brooker, 'Paolo Manutio's use of fore-edge titles for presentation copies (1540–1541)', in *The Book Collector* XLVI, 1997, pp. 27–68; pp.193–209.

C.J. Weber, *A Thousand and One Fore–edge Paintings*, Waterville, 1949. [This volume is well-illustrated but many of the attributions are incorrect.]

Structure and techniques

D. de Bray, *A short instruction in the binding of books by de Bray followed by a note on the gilding of the edges by Ambrosius Vermerck*, Amsterdam, 1977. [A translation of a manual written and illustrated by a seventeenth-century Dutch apprentice.]

J.A. Arnett (pseud. for John Harnett), *Bibliopegia; or the Art of Bookbinding in all its Branches*, London, 1835.

E. Diehl, *Bookbinding; Its Background and Technique*, 2 vols., New York, 1946, reprinted New York & London, 1980.

B.C. Middleton, *A History of English Craft Bookbinding Technique*, 4th edition, London, 1996.

N. Pickwood, 'The Interpretation of Bookbinding Structure', in *The Library*, 6th series, 17, 1995, 211–249.

N. Pickwood, 'Onward and downward' in R. Myers & M. Harris, (eds.), *A Millenium of the Book*, Winchester, 1994, pp. 61–106.

G. Pollard, 'Changes in the style of bookbinding 1550–1830', in *The Library*, 5th series, XI, 1956, 71–79.

G. Pollard & E. Potter, *Early Bookbinding Manuals; An annotated list of Technical Accounts of Bookbinding to 1840*, Oxford, 1984.

J.A. Szirmai, 'Archaeology of bookbinding', in *Quaerendo*, 27, 1996, 410–429.

Journal articles

Periodicals which feature articles on bookbinding include:
The Book Collector, London, 1952–
The British Library Journal, London, 1975–
The British Museum Quarterly, London, 1926–74
Bulletin du Bibliophile, Paris, 1834–
Gutenberg-Jahrbuch, Mainz, 1926–
The Library, London, [formerly Transactions of the Bibliographical Society, 1892–]
Proceedings and papers of the Bibliographical Society of America, New York, 1906–
The New Bookbinder, London, 1981– [formerly known as the *Designer Bookbinders' Review*, London, 1973–79]

Conservation matters are discussed in
The Abbey Newsletter, New York, 1976–
Library Conservation News, London, 1983– [a newsletter produced by the National Preservation Office, the British Library]

Index